Jeremy S. Gaies, Psy.D.
and James B. Morris, Jr., Ph.D.

MINDFUL CO-PARENTING:

A Child-Friendly Path through Divorce

Acknowledgements

Books don't just happen. This book was born from our mutual passion for helping families find a peaceful path through divorce. Although we love our face-to-face work with families, we often find ourselves wishing we could reach a wider audience. Thus the book.

Each of us is blessed with a loving wife and two wonderful daughters. We are tremendously grateful for their constant support. Without it, we would not be able to devote ourselves so fully to the fascinating and rewarding field within which we work.

We also thank our colleagues who have generously shared their wisdom with us. Working with divorcing and divorced parents has introduced us to a diverse set of professionals that includes family law attorneys, financial experts, mediators, and fellow mental health professionals. One of the unexpected benefits for us has been the development of wonderful friendships and a rich and varied professional community.

Finally, we want to express how much we value the families that come to us and allow us to be part of their lives. They teach us what the experience of divorce feels like, and they stimulate our thinking about our roles as advocates and helpers. It is from these families that we have learned the most, and we thank them for that.

Table of Contents

one

Mindfulness Matters

A few years back, there was a video circulating on the Internet in which a group of college students were dribbling and passing basketballs among themselves. At the start of the video, the viewer was asked to count the number of passes. At the end of the video, the viewer was told the correct number of passes and then was asked, "But did you see the gorilla?!" Sure enough, when viewers watched the video again, they could see that a person in a gorilla suit walked right through the group of college students. It is almost unfathomable that viewers would not notice the gorilla the first time, but most people missed it altogether.

The reality is that we miss all kinds of things happening around us throughout our daily lives. This can occur when we focus our attention on something we believe to be important, or when we are distracted by something that we know is not important. In either case, we focus on certain things and overlook others. In and of itself, that is not a problem. We cannot possibly pay attention to everything around us all of the time. The fact that we fail to see the gorilla in the video is not a problem; what is a problem is not seeing something that really does matter. It is a serious problem when we fail to attend to those things that affect our health, our relationships, and our other life priorities.

Most parents would affirm that how we raise our children is a top priority, but parents who are going through a divorce may have a hard time staying on track. Divorce stirs up a swarm of issues, each of which cries out for attention. Legal, emotional, financial, and social concerns—all of these can assault parents, especially in high-conflict divorces. These challenges begin when parents make the decision to end their marriage, but they do not end when the divorce decree is signed. The need for thoughtful parenting goes on at least until the children are no longer in the home, and it may extend into the children's early years of adulthood.

In this book, we focus on a construct we call *mindful co-parenting*. *Co-parenting* refers to the ways that you and your children's other parent relate to one another in regard to raising your children when you are no longer in a committed relationship as a *couple*.[1] When you divorce you are still in a committed relationship, but that commitment is to the children, not to one another. You and your former partner are no longer a couple, but you are both still your children's family.

What we mean by the term *mindful* is a bit more involved. Some people are skeptical when we speak of mindfulness; to them, the concept seems abstract, or it evokes an image of a person sitting cross-legged pursuing a form of mystical meditation. But mindfulness is actually quite practical and down-to-earth. Jon Kabat-Zinn, in his book *Wherever You Go, There You Are* (1994) wrote, "Mindfulness means paying attention in a particular way: on purpose, in the present moment and non-judgmentally. This kind of attention nurtures greater awareness, clarity, and acceptance of present-moment reality. It wakes us up to the fact that our lives unfold only in moments. If we are not fully present for many of those moments, we may not only miss what is most valuable in our lives but also fail to realize the richness and the depth of our possibilities for

---

1 Throughout this book, we refer to committed relationships that produce one or more children as a *marriage*. We refer to the end of such relationships as a *divorce*. In reality, many people in committed relationships who have children are not officially married, and if their relationships end, those are not technically divorces. We use the terms marriage and divorce, however, for the sake of simplicity. We think that many of the concepts shared in this book are fully applicable to committed couples with children, who were never married, and whose relationship as a couple ended. Some of the principles will also apply to individuals who were never a couple, but who produced a child together and share parenting responsibilities.

growth and transformation" (p. 4). Being mindful keeps us focused on how we can deal with each moment in the most adaptive way and keeps us from letting our unconscious anger, resentment, fear, or learned habits interfere with our efforts to live a happy life. It is a way to observe ourselves at a meaningful level, to evaluate our actions in terms of our most strongly held values, and to behave in an effective manner. As Kabat-Zinn describes it, mindfulness is simply "the art of conscious living."

Mindful co-parenting is about paying attention to the choices that arise in helping your children through the divorce process and working with your co-parent to raise your children to be healthy, happy, and fulfilled. You will face many decisions over the course of your children's lives. These choices will include such things as when the children are to be with each parent, how to establish a consistent bedtime and other rules between two homes, and which decisions you will make jointly with your co-parent versus those that you will each make unilaterally. In later years, these choices might include how to jointly shepherd your children through the transition from teenagers to young adults, how to support their passages through college and beyond, and how to find peaceful coexistence with your ex-spouse as your children marry and begin their own families. Being fully aware and focused on your priorities will help you to navigate all of these choices in the best ways possible.

> *Mindful co-parenting is our term for paying attention to how you parent your children along with your children's other parent—day by day, moment by moment, and with a focus on what is in the long-term best interest of your children.*

Mindful co-parenting is simple, but it is not easy. We believe that mindful co-parenting begins with your decision about divorce. That decision is an enormous one, so it requires careful consideration of how it will impact you as parents and how it will affect your children. Once the decision to divorce is made, you must then decide specifically how to proceed through the divorce process and how to structure your co-parenting relationship. This is followed by creating a long-term plan for co-parenting, one that defines how you will share the tasks of decision making and how you will share time with your children. Finally, mindful co-parenting is about how to develop a new relationship with your co-parent as a partner in the most important project in your lives: raising your children to have the brightest futures possible.

two

Making the Decision to Divorce

Should I stay or should I go now?
If I go there will be trouble
An' if I stay it will be double
So you gotta let me know
Should I stay or should I go?

These lines from the 1982 song by the British rock band The Clash capture the dilemma that spouses face when confronted with questions about whether it makes sense to divorce. The consequences of remaining in a marriage or leaving a marriage can be both positive and negative, having profound effects on multiple aspects of life for parents and children. In some cases, the benefits of staying in a marriage outweigh the benefits of leaving, while in other cases the benefits of ending a marriage prevail. In either case, these consequences will be multilayered and long lasting, especially for families with very young children.

Choosing to divorce is especially difficult when it is unclear whether divorcing will improve the lives of your children or make their lives less happy or less safe. Many parents base their decisions about divorce on the best interests of their children, but it is not always evident which path will better serve the children's needs. Staying together in an unhappy marriage may mean that children grow up in an unhappy family. This could affect how children learn to view relationships, which could have a negative impact on their own future partnering. However, if parents who stay together in these marriages do a good job of insulating the children from their conflict and treat one another with respect, the children may end up relatively unscathed. For some families, on the other hand, divorce is the best option for the well-being of the children. As we will discuss in depth in Chapter 5, if parents manage certain factors well during and after a divorce, the long-term outcomes for children can be favorable.

The decision to divorce is complicated when divorce conflicts with a parent's personal values, such as when a parent's religious beliefs prohibit divorce or when a parent feels a moral obligation to stay with a spouse due to that spouse's physical, emotional, or financial needs. Finances become particularly relevant when resources are insufficient to provide for two homes. If one or both parents have limited social support, this too may influence the ultimate decision about divorce.

Other complicating factors may include one parent being pressured to stay in the marriage, especially if the other parent is dominant and controlling. In addition, the decision to divorce is difficult for parents who do not have confidence in their ability to function independently. Low self-esteem, limited education, poor job skills, inadequate financial or social resources, or problems with depression, anxiety, or substance abuse may all lead a parent to feel overwhelmed at the prospect of being on his or her own. When domestic violence or emotional abuse of a spouse has been present, a parent may want to escape the marriage but may struggle over how to leave in a safe way. That parent may also fear for the safety of the children if he or she were to leave the marriage, as the other parent may be awarded time with the children after the marriage ends.

Making the decision to divorce can be gut-wrenching, but in some cases it is the only reasonable option. When the incompatibilities between spouses are vast and the level of conflict or hostility is high and cannot be resolved, staying together is destructive. Divorce may also be the obvious outcome when one or both spouses become involved in another relationship, or when one partner is so lost in drug abuse or mental illness that recovery is unlikely. Sometimes a marriage is ended to save a spouse; sometimes it is ended to save the children. We would never suggest that these divorces are without pain, even when the decision is an inevitable one. Under these circumstances, however, the decision is likely to be more straightforward for the spouse choosing to end the marriage.

Prior to making a final decision about divorce, some parents consider the option of a trial separation. Although undergoing such a separation may be a sensible measure to take before parents make a formal and permanent decision about ending the marriage, its value depends greatly on the couple and hinges on their thoughts and feelings regarding the marriage. Marie and Joe are a good example of a couple exploring this question:

> Marie sat in the therapist's office with her husband and softly said, "Joe, it's just not going to work. We've tried and tried, but it's not right for me, it's not right for you, and we can't make it right for the kids. I think it's time that we face facts."
>
> Joe appeared both angry and scared. "How can you do this? A divorce will be bad for the kids and you know it! Let's take it slow. What if I move in with my brother for a couple of weeks and see what happens?"
>
> Marie didn't reply, so the therapist asked, "Marie, is it possible that taking some time apart might change your feelings?"
>
> Marie quickly and decisively shook her head from side to side. "No," she answered, "it will not change my mind. It's time for us to divorce."

It seems clear that this couple is not a good candidate for a trial separation, as one spouse (in this case, the wife) has already decided that she is not willing to consider the possibility of reconciliation. In other cases, however, the conversation goes quite differently. In an office just down the street, another couple is having a similar conversation, but with a different outcome.

> *Patty turned to her husband, Frank, and said, "I just want to do what's right for the kids. I don't know if we can make this work, but I'd like to try."*
>
> *Frank nodded. "You know, there's not a whole lot that we've been agreeing on, but I'm with you on this one. I'm not sure what will happen if we spend some time living apart—or even what I want to happen—but I definitely think we owe it to ourselves and to our kids. Let's do our best and give it a few months."*

There are pros and cons to having a period of separation. Separation can be a useful intermediate step between marriage and divorce. It allows couples to explore the viability of their marriage before taking formal steps toward divorce. It often answers questions that need to be answered in order for a couple to proceed either to reconciliation or to the ending of their marriage. The most important benefit is that it may allow a couple more emotional and physical space while working through their issues, typically with the help of a therapist. If a couple is able to resurrect their marriage by taking time apart, then everyone in the family has a favorable outcome. A second benefit of separation is that if the couple eventually proceeds to divorce, it offers both spouses a period of transition to separate their lives while providing a more gradual transitioning for the children to separate homes.

There can be downsides to separation, however. A separation that does not involve active work on the relationship is unlikely to result in an improvement in the marriage; this can set up the whole family for disappointment. If a separation is not time-limited and goes on and on without resolution, one or both spouses may become frustrated and angry. This can lead to greater resentment between the two, especially when one spouse strongly wants the marriage to survive and the separation ultimately leads to divorce. It is not uncommon that a spouse agrees to a period of separation only because he or she feels forced into it, and that spouse may develop hostility toward the other during the separation. Last, a gradual move toward an inevitable divorce can be like slowly pulling off a Band-Aid. Rather than quickly dealing with a painful event, it drags the pain out over a longer period of time and causes more suffering than necessary for the spouse who is less motivated to end the marriage. It can also cause more disruption, confusion, and uncertainty for the children.

Given the pros and cons, how then should couples decide whether to agree to a trial separation? Ideally, couples will consider the following five questions:

1. Do you both want the marriage to work?
2. Do you both believe that it is possible for the marriage to work?
3. Are you both willing to make meaningful changes in yourselves to make the marriage work?
4. Does at least one of you believe that taking some time apart is necessary in order to resolve the problems between you?
5. Are you both willing to actively work on improving the marriage (presumably with a marriage therapist) throughout a predetermined period of separation?

If both spouses answer affirmatively to all five of these questions, then a period of separation is highly likely to be helpful. Negative answers would indicate that a separation is not the right choice. When there is a risk to the physical or emotional safety of a parent or a child, an immediate separation is recommended, with other matters being addressed after the separation has begun.[2]

---

2 If there is actual or threatened physical violence in the home, then the process of leaving, and the immediate aftermath of leaving, may both be times of danger for the departing parent or the children. In these situations, we strongly recommend that a professional with expertise in domestic violence issues be consulted for guidance and support.

If a couple decides that a separation would be appropriate and safety issues are not a concern, the separation should occur only after a plan is in place for how the parents will share time with the children and how other matters affecting the family will be handled. During the separation, both parents are still parents, and coordination of co-parenting is critical. Good co-parenting is necessary to help the children cope with such a major change in the family. How the parents handle this period is a good measure of how they will handle these issues in the future. Successful co-parenting during separation affirms for parents that they will be able to work as a team on their children's behalf if a divorce does occur.

While the length of the separation depends on the specific circumstances of the family, it is our experience that a period of three to six months is appropriate to achieve the goal of determining if the marriage should continue. A period shorter than three months may not be a sufficient test of what it feels like to live separately, and it is not long enough to expect marriage therapy to resolve the couple's issues. On the other hand, a period greater than six months is rarely necessary. With few exceptions, if parents are unable to decide on the fate of their marriage within six months, it is unlikely that they will gain clarity just by taking a larger amount of time apart. There is also a danger inherent to overextending a separation, as it may lead both spouses to stay stuck in marital limbo.

When a couple with children decides to separate, it is essential that each parent continues to play an active role in the children's lives. If one parent has previously played a peripheral role, it becomes important for that parent's role to increase in order to ensure that he or she does not become fully absent. Sadly, in some families, when one parent moves out of the home, that parent begins to disappear from the children's lives. This outcome may result from a variety of factors. There may be a lack of effort on the part of a parent, or there may be a lack of availability, such as when one parent lives far from the marital home. A parent may also be "made to disappear" by the parent with whom the children spend the majority of the time. If that parent is angry or resentful, he or she may create obstacles that keep the other parent from spending much time with the children. These obstructionist actions on the part of one parent are referred to by professionals in the field as *restrictive gatekeeping* and can be a major problem for families of divorce—and a poor choice for the children.

If both parents had active roles before the temporary separation, the goal is to maintain those active roles. The children should have frequent time with both parents, and schedules should be handled in a way that both parents are involved with as many aspects of the children's lives as possible, especially those that were routine in the past. For example, a Dad who reads a bedtime story to the children every night might still be able to do so during the trial separation, even if it must occur by phone. Likewise, a Mom who always drives her daughter to dance class might still be able to do so despite the circumstances. When a divorce takes place, some of these routines must flex, but during a temporary separation, it is best to keep practices as much the same as possible for the sake of the children. What is meant to change during a separation is that the parents interact less with each other, not that the parents interact less with the children.

When a decision is made to separate, it is necessary to share that decision with the children. Children should be informed once the parents have agreed on a plan and worked out the details. The discussion with the children should occur no sooner than about a month before one parent moves to a new residence and no later than a couple of weeks before. These time frames allow the children time to process the news before actual changes take place but without an excessive amount of time spent anticipating the move. If a child is moving out with a parent, which is a less common situation, then more time is needed. Ideally, the parents should talk to the children together. They should present this decision in a calm, rational manner, with a shared explanation of the reasons for the separation and a plan for how the family will deal with the separation. If the level of conflict between the parents is so high that they cannot perform this task cooperatively, however, then a joint conversation with the children is not advisable. In that case, the parents should individually discuss the decision with the children. In doing so, they must be sure that the overall message is similar and in no way casts blame on either parent. The conversation(s) will typically require only about ten to fifteen minutes and must answer a few key questions from the child's perspective:

1. What is happening?
2. Is it my fault and can I fix it?
3. Who is going to take care of me?

Children do not need a great deal of information, and the truth is that most children do not want to know details about their parents' relationship problems. While there are exceptions to this rule—some children appear to want to know *everything*—this does not mean that those children should be given the details. While we always want to address children's questions, we need to be mindful that too much information can be confusing, burdensome, and inappropriate. Basically, what children need to know is that Mom and Dad love them. Address the reasons for the separation as simply and as positively as possible, only sharing the reasons the children already know—e.g., Mom and Dad have been arguing and not getting along. Tell the children that Mom and Dad are going to try living in two different homes for a few months because they hope this will help them to figure out how they can work better together. Focus on some positive aspects of having two homes that might counterbalance the more negative implications of this decision. Sometimes ideas such as, "Let's decorate your new room this weekend!" or "Won't it be fun to go to the playground in the new apartment complex?" give a child something to look forward to.

Children need to know what will stay the same. In a separation, most things do stay the same except that one parent will be living in a different place and the children will spend time with each parent on a particular schedule. Children also need to know that Mom and Dad's decision to spend time apart is not in any way the children's fault, that there is nothing the children could have done differently that would have changed this decision, and that there is nothing they can do to change it now.

Children also need to know that both Mom and Dad are going to continue to take care of them. Youngsters sometimes ask if their parents might decide to separate from them in the same way they have decided to separate from each other, and it is essential that both parents convey this message loud and clear: While we may decide to separate from each other, we will not ever separate from you or abandon you! It is exceptionally important during the period of separation that both parents remain very actively involved in the children's lives and that the children know they can easily and regularly contact their parents. By providing all of this information to children, parents effectively answer the three critical questions previously listed and help prepare the children for the separation.

During the separation, the parents should not discuss with the children all of the possibilities of what might happen. While children may well ask about the likelihood of reconciliation or divorce, these are questions that the parents are unlikely to be able to answer with any certainty. When a parent begins to get a sense of the prognosis for the marriage, this topic needs to be discussed with the other parent and then jointly addressed with the children at the appropriate time.

Many parents find that a period of separation is an ideal time to seek guidance and support from a therapist who specializes in helping families through such periods of change. They may seek help as individuals, as a couple, or as a family unit. In addition, children may benefit from having someone outside the family with whom they can share their feelings about the changes the family is undergoing. When a child is displaying any symptoms of distress, such as notable sadness, anxiety, fear, anger, misbehavior, or school problems, then a therapist should be considered to help the child cope with the changes. Even if the symptoms are mild, it is likely that involving a therapist, for at least a few sessions, will help mitigate the challenges the child faces. While some parents are hesitant to have their children meet with a therapist, there is very little risk to allowing a few sessions. Preventing larger problems for the children is an important task during this transitional period. School counselors may also be helpful, and some progressive school systems offer programs designed for children whose parents are separated or divorcing.

Realistically, the majority of couples who have a trial separation do not return to their marriages; in fact, some studies suggest that only about ten percent of separating couples eventually reconcile. Thus, we should have sober expectations about the likelihood that a marriage will continue beyond a separation. Still, trial separations do save some marriages, and the number of children who are positively affected as a result is quite large. There are over a million divorces that take place in the United States and Canada each year. If you consider that many families have two children or more, even with only ten percent of separating couples ultimately reconciling, that is still a staggering number of children who may benefit from trial separations. At a personal level, if your family is one of those families that was helped, how much might that mean to you?

Regardless of whether a separation occurs, a couple struggling with the question of divorce must ultimately make a final decision. There is no magic formula for a decision like this and no absolute guidelines to follow. There are, however, some commonsense approaches to making this decision. First, try to distinguish facts from feelings. Critical decisions require a careful examination of objective realities, so take an honest look at the facts without being influenced by your emotions. Identify the problems in your marriage, the options for resolving them, the attempts that you have made to date, the motivation evidenced by each of you to work on a resolution, and the likelihood of fixing the problems. Some parents apply the tried-and-true technique of listing the pros and cons to help with their analysis, and this might be worth trying.

Another approach to processing this decision is to discuss it with one or more trusted people in your life, such as a relative, a close friend, a clergy member, or a professional counselor, all of whom may offer helpful guidance. This is one of the most meaningful decisions you are likely to make in your lifetime and it therefore deserves as much input as can be found. This is not to say that divorcing spouses should not discuss the decision with each other. Assuming there is still a trusting relationship, they should talk about these things together, but each spouse should also seek objective advisors. Talking with a friend who has always disliked your spouse is not what we have in mind. Seek out impartial, caring people who understand you, understand what divorce will mean for you and your children, and who are not unfairly biased for one choice or the other.

In addition to these approaches, do whatever you need to do to explore your feelings. Some people find that writing out their thoughts and emotions helps a great deal, and keeping a journal for a period of time can be useful. Other people find that taking some time on their own, either a day at the beach, a weekend in the mountains, or a week in the city, helps to clarify their thinking. However you go about this exploration, be mindful of the ways in which the divorce will affect the children. While children's needs should not be the only determining factor, it is your responsibility as a parent to give their needs special weight.

Ultimately, most parents know when they are ready to divorce, as painful, saddening, and anxiety-provoking as it may be. Earlier in this chapter we discussed the principles of telling children about a separation. The recommendations for informing children about divorce are basically the same, though there are some distinct nuances. When parents are separating, there is an implicit assumption that they are still working together and have some hope of the relationship working out. With the decision to divorce, however, there is a sense of finality that may make it harder for them to work together. But communicating effectively and managing this conversation with the children is worth significant effort. Children will always remember the moment when they learned that their parents were planning to divorce.

It is best when parents can present a united front when disclosing the decision to divorce to the children. If the parents are not able to be together when doing this, it becomes all the more important that they coordinate their separate efforts. What and when will each parent tell the children? Make sure you are consistent in the timing and information you present. Even if you are not conveying the information at the same place and at the same time, let your children know that it is a mutual plan, one to which both parents have agreed. If one of you does not want the divorce, we are not asking you to be dishonest. Simply state it objectively, such as, "Mommy and Daddy are getting a divorce" as opposed to, "Daddy has decided to divorce Mommy." During a divorce, children frequently fear losing the chance to spend time with one parent or the other. If one parent discloses that the divorce is the choice of the other parent, a child may become anxious that the parent who chose to leave the marriage will eventually leave him or her as well. Hearing one parent blame the other can also lead a child to side with one parent or the other, which is never in a child's best interest.

We recommend that you be honest about why you are getting divorced, but that does not mean you need to share all the details with your children. Adjust your message to their ages; young children need less information, while older children may need a bit more. Focus on the answers to the three core questions raised earlier in this chapter, concerning what is changing in the family, that it is not your children's fault, and how Dad and Mom will continue to take care of them. Avoid any comments that might encourage your children to side with you. It is not a competition, and when you try to gain your children's favor, the children become the primary losers. If you feel the need for vindication, seek that from close adult friends and do so in a manner that will not expose your children to your negative views about your spouse.

Reassure your children that the divorce does not change your love for them. Realistically acknowledge the changes that are going to be taking place, but try to do so in a way that emphasizes the positive aspects of those changes. Be sure that your children know that they were not responsible for the divorce in any way and that there was nothing they could have done differently to have kept the marriage together.

Do your best to present the information in a calm, non-emotional manner. It will not help your children to see you break down and cry while you talk about this. It may help to visualize speaking with your children and to practice the material in your head prior to the conversation so that you are not caught off guard by your own emotional reactions when you begin talking to them. If your children seem to be significantly distressed afterward and are not bouncing back as you might have expected or hoped, consider that this may be the time to consult a school counselor or a child therapist who specializes in divorce issues.

Once the decision to divorce is made, a new stage begins: the process of divorce itself. As with all aspects of mindful co-parenting, we will examine this next step with a focus on the impact on the children.

three

Choosing a Child-Focused Divorce

The next step in the divorce process is to determine *how* you will get divorced. There are different ways to end a marriage, some of which are more child-focused than others. You should carefully consider which of these approaches will be best for you and your family. We will start by describing the traditional method of divorce and then outline four alternatives, each of which may offer important benefits for you and your children.

Traditional Litigation

The term *litigation* may refer to a criminal trial or, in civil court, to bringing a lawsuit against someone. While the term litigation does not strictly imply that attorneys are involved, we use the term *traditional litigation* to refer to a process in which there are two distinct sides to an issue, each side hires one or more attorneys, and the sides present their arguments in an adversarial manner before a court. After hearing from each side, the court determines the outcome. This approach may be effective for dealing with many issues, but it is not friendly to families.

When a marriage is dissolved via traditional litigation, the spouses engage in a legal battle against one another to advance their wishes regarding parenting time, shared financial assets, and continuing financial support. Their attorneys present evidence to convince the judge to decide in favor of one spouse or the other. Litigation involves many things that are complicated, confusing, and frightening for the average person, such as subpoenas, depositions, court hearings, cross-examination, and expert testimony. Interestingly, at the end of an often brutal and costly process, most couples end up settling out of court, i.e., prior to the trial. A relatively small percentage of cases, however, do go to trial, and a judge makes the final decisions.

Whether cases settle or go to trial, spouses spend a tremendous amount of money due to the involvement of attorneys, experts, and the pursuit of all of the required legal processes. Litigated divorces are always expensive, and they can be very, very expensive. They are also long and drawn-out, with the average divorce taking almost a year-and-a-half to complete. When matters are complicated and the volume of cases overwhelms courts, it can take years for divorces to be resolved.

Another drawback of litigated divorces is that they tend to escalate conflict and destroy any good will remaining between the spouses, thereby crippling the co-parenting relationship. Litigation takes decision making out of the hands of the parents—the people who we believe should be making choices for the children—and puts it in the hands of a judge who has both limited time and limited information to make decisions that will impact the lives of each of the family members for years to come.

Despite all of these concerns, however, there is a place for litigated divorce. If one parent rigidly insists on an unreasonable parenting plan and fights any attempt at a compromise, then the other parent has little choice but to fight back on behalf of the children. For example, if one parent insists on having the children the vast majority of time despite the other parent being caring, competent, and highly involved, then litigation may be needed. Another example is when a parent with serious mental health issues or substance use problems insists on having the children half of the time. Litigation also may be the only way to ensure an even playing field when there is a considerable power imbalance between the spouses. An example of this is when one spouse is extremely controlling or abusive and the other spouse feels so intimidated that he or she is unable to speak up assertively over the course of the divorce process. When these types of conditions are not present, however, alternatives to traditional, adversarial litigation are almost always the better choice.

A Pro Se Divorce

The first alternative to traditional litigation is one in which you and your spouse navigate the legal system on your own. When a divorce is conducted without attorneys, it is referred to in the legal world as a *pro se* divorce, which is Latin for "for oneself" or "on one's own behalf." Simply put, it refers to an individual representing oneself in a legal dispute. A pro se divorce may be adversarial, similar to a traditional, litigated divorce that involves attorneys, but if both spouses are seeking a peaceful resolution, then a pro se divorce can be cooperative. A cooperative pro se divorce requires a certain level of trust between spouses and a mutual commitment to work amicably toward a final resolution. In this process, you and your spouse try to reach an agreement on all matters, including a parenting plan, a division of marital assets, and spousal support, which is commonly referred to as alimony.[3] By reaching a comprehensive settlement on your own, you can substantially minimize the amount of time and money you might otherwise spend. Once again, however, this approach to divorce depends on a relatively high level of trust and a willingness to reach an agreement without excessive conflict. Thus, a pro se divorce is not suitable for every family.

Even if you and your soon-to-be "ex" believe that you can work through all the issues without hiring attorneys to represent you, you might still choose to use an attorney in one of two ways. The first way would be to consult with an attorney just to learn about your legal rights and what you might expect from the divorce process prior to trying to

---

3 Child support falls into a different category, as it is generally determined by a standard formula, so there may not be much to negotiate when it comes to this decision. This formula is typically based on how much time the children spend with each parent and how much money each parent earns.

work out an agreement with your spouse. This type of consultation can help you understand what your options might be if the pro se negotiations do not succeed. The second way of using an attorney in a pro se case would be to have two separate attorneys (one for each spouse) or one mutually selected attorney to review the agreements you have reached and to confirm that the language used in those agreements is legally sound. If a shared attorney is used, that attorney would not be retained to represent either spouse, but would provide legal guidance as a consultant.

Hiring Solution-Oriented Attorneys

A second alternative to traditional litigation is for each spouse to hire a non-adversarial, solution-oriented attorney to negotiate the settlement and help work through disputes that might otherwise block an agreement. Divorces that are resolved by solution-oriented attorneys are often referred to as *cooperative divorces*. The key to this type of divorce is finding the right attorneys. If both attorneys are focused on finding mutually acceptable solutions and are committed to minimizing contentious interactions, then the process can be relatively amicable and efficient.

We view cooperative divorces far more favorably than traditionally litigated divorces, as settlements are reached with considerably less damage to families and with considerably less cost. Cooperative or solution-oriented divorces are also a better choice than a pro se divorce when there are complex issues to resolve, such as when a couple owns a business together or when it is not clear which assets the couple own together versus separately. Having the right attorney can go a long way toward ensuring that the parties are making reasonable and legally sound decisions. Hiring the wrong attorney, however, can cause big problems. If one or both of the attorneys (or one or both parents) focus on winning rather than on workable solutions, the process will become adversarial, and it then devolves into a traditional, litigated divorce. If the case cannot be brought back onto a cooperative track, the family may find itself in an escalating battle, which is seldom the best path.

Mediation

A third alternative for reaching a settlement in a non-adversarial way is through mediation. Mediation is one of the more civilized and peaceful approaches to resolving disputes. In a typical mediation session focused on the dissolution of a marriage, an impartial professional with special training works with the spouses to help them reach a mutually acceptable divorce agreement. A mediation session, which lasts from several hours to all day, may occur with or without the participation of attorneys. As a result, mediation can be used either for pro se divorces or for divorces in which one or both spouses hire legal counsel. The cost of mediation is generally moderate, although the costs rise if attorneys are present and if the divorce is more complicated. In some cases, multiple mediation sessions are required in order to address all of the family's issues. Many jurisdictions now require that mediation be attempted for all divorces because it is so successful at producing settlements and preventing the need for lengthy trials in front of a judge. Mediation can be helpful even if some issues cannot be resolved. The more disputes that can be resolved prior to going to court, the fewer there will be for the court to address.

Collaborative Divorce

A fourth option designed to help parents reach their own settlement is called *collaborative divorce*. Collaborative divorce involves a team of professionals working with both spouses together to craft a divorce agreement that is fair and that fulfills the interests of both the spouses and their children. There are several models for collaborative divorce that use different combinations of professionals. The goal is to identify the model that is the best fit for the family in question. Though we have each used different models, we prefer one that consists of a team made up of two attorneys and two neutral professionals. In this model, each attorney represents one spouse, and the neutral professionals are a mental health specialist, who serves as the facilitator, and a financial expert, who gathers, organizes, and explains the financial data. Regardless of the model selected, the process almost always benefits from the team-work and collegiality that are inherent in the collaborative approach.

In our opinion, the biggest benefit of collaborative divorce is its success in achieving positive outcomes for children and their families. In collaborative cases, there is a very high likelihood of reaching an agreement, with national surveys reflecting a success rate of 85% to 90%. There is also a greater likelihood of preserving a positive, postdivorce relationship between the parents and thus a better ability to co-parent after the divorce. Collaborative divorces tend to avoid the conflict and hostility that arise in other approaches. This calmer, more peaceful tone protects both the spouses and the children in the family. The collaborative process allows parents to think outside the box in designing a creative and detailed agreement that addresses the children's emotional and financial needs.

A collaborative divorce is also the most private form of divorce, as the activities of the divorce occur behind closed doors and outside the semi-public venue of the courthouse. Spouses do not have to appear at multiple court hearings. Many jurisdictions allow the parties to file only the final agreement and a basic financial summary, as opposed to the full financial disclosure that is required in non-collaborative divorces.

Using a team of professionals means that collaborative divorces are not cheap, but they are often a good value due to their relative efficiency and positive outcomes. In some cases, a collaborative divorce can actually save a family a great deal of money. The savings come from avoiding the costs of traditional litigation, which eliminates the need to have attorneys file motions and countermotions, conduct depositions, hire separate financial experts, and pursue expensive courtroom battles. One reason collaborative divorce is so successful is due to what is known as the "disqualification rule". This rule dictates that if the process does not reach a final agreement, both attorneys are barred from continued representation of the parents if the case goes to court. This encourages everyone to remain at the table working to reach an agreement.

సాళ

In summary, there are five approaches to divorce, including traditional litigation and four alternatives. Mediation and collaborative divorce are usually far less hostile and cause less damage than traditionally litigated divorces. Cooperative divorce is often a good option, but only if the spouses and the attorneys are truly settlement oriented and committed to staying that way. Traditional litigation is clearly the least family friendly and should be reserved for the relatively few cases that require it.

Which approach is best for your family? This decision depends largely on each spouse's circumstances and whether there can be a shared commitment that both of them will avoid unnecessary conflict throughout the divorce process. The higher-conflict approaches take an emotional, physical, and financial toll, while the lower-conflict approaches allow you to devote your energy to your life ahead, including your parenting, your health, your career, and your future relationships. By ending your marriage in a manner that fosters a workable co-parenting relationship, you save yourself and your children years of discord. These less conflictual options reduce the likelihood that your children will suffer collateral damage, and avoiding a financial blowout preserves funds for your children's current and future needs. For all of these reasons, we strongly recommend that you make every possible effort to pursue one of the lower conflict, more child-focused approaches to divorce.

Child-focused divorces, in our opinion, are mindful divorces. The decision to divorce and the approach selected are choices that should reflect your deepest values. We suspect that you hold the well-being of your children as your highest priority. Therefore, your chosen path through the divorce process should honor that priority. If you believe that the well-being of your children requires you to pursue traditional litigation, then do so — but be aware of any hidden motivations. Ask yourself if your pursuit of litigation might be about being angry, wanting to hurt your ex-partner, or just wanting to fight, rather than protecting your children. If you believe that maintaining a calm, peaceful, and functional relationship with your children's other parent is possible, then a more child-friendly approach should be pursued. We cannot tell you which approach is right for you, as we do not know your family's unique circumstances, but we advise you to make the choice mindfully, aware of the values that you hold dear and that are centered on what is best for your children.

Where to Learn More

Identifying the legal option that is right for you will require some research. Detailed information is available in books, magazine and newspaper articles, and through the Internet. You can also obtain information by talking to people who have gone through their own divorces and by talking to the professionals with whom you might consider working. Many attorneys, mediators, and collaborative professionals offer free initial consultations. Another good way to get a lot of information is by meeting with a divorce counselor or a divorce coach to discuss your options. Many employers offer an Employee Assistance Program (EAP) that provides a number of free sessions with attorneys and/or counselors to employees and their dependents.

four

How Divorce Affects You as a Parent

The technical term used for divorce is the *dissolution of marriage*. Dissolution means that something dissolves, and when we think of something dissolving, such as sugar in warm water, we picture it gradually and quietly disappearing from sight. Unfortunately, this is not even close to the experience that most families have when a marriage ends. Divorce is not a quiet and peaceful dissolving, but rather a process with ups and downs, with periods of conflict and chaos, and with notable disruption to many aspects of each family member's life.

Divorce is full of emotion, including anger, hurt, frustration, sadness, relief, hope, fear, and guilt. Indeed, there are few losses as pervasive, especially when there are children involved. Many divorces trigger deeply felt grief in the family members, sometimes even in the spouse who is more in favor of the divorce. According to the classic grief model proposed by Dr. Elisabeth Kübler-Ross in 1969, people experiencing grief move through stages of denial, anger, bargaining, depression, and then acceptance. While we now view the grief process as being more complex and variable than this model might imply, it is clear that any serious loss, including the loss of a marriage, will bring with it a range of intense emotions. And while these emotions do gradually soften for the vast majority of people, they can last for some time. We have found that it takes about two years on average to fully recover from the psychological effects of a divorce. If it is a high-conflict divorce, recovery may take much longer. Of course, everyone is different, and some people heal more quickly than these figures would suggest, but the point is that the emotional impact of divorce is powerful, and it takes time to work through all of the feelings it evokes.

Divorce also changes the experience of being a parent. When spouses separate, they almost always divide time with the children in some manner, so each parent must learn to live for periods of time without direct physical interaction with their children. Different parents react to these absences in different ways. For some, it remains the most painful part of the divorce, as those days and nights separated from their children can be wrenching. For others, these periods are difficult at first, but the discomfort softens over time as they learn to tolerate the absences. In addition to dealing with absences from the children, each parent must learn how to spend extended periods of time caring for the children without the support or assistance of the other parent. When they are each with the children for these blocks of time, they face demands much like those faced by a single parent. If one parent has the lion's share of the parenting time, the responsibility can be overwhelming. The challenge may also be great for a parent who is not used to handling the daily tasks of making lunches, getting children to school, driving the carpool, helping kids with homework, and making dinner. Suddenly becoming a part-time, solo parent is especially difficult when the other parent is unsupportive, unreliable, or hostile.

The financial responsibilities can be extremely challenging as well. Some parents end up having to provide for their children with limited support from the other parent. Even when both parents do their best to provide financially for the family's needs, the ends do not always meet. Resources that may have been adequate when the family lived together in one home may not cover all the costs of living in two separate homes. Financial stress may also increase because of costs associated with the divorce, especially if litigation is involved.

Money plays a complicated role in divorce; it can be a blessing and a curse. Some families have limited financial resources but manage to use them wisely during a divorce, obtaining enough professional help to ensure that they have a mutually acceptable final agreement. Other families have huge financial resources that may become weapons to use against one another, costing the family inordinate amounts and potentially squandering assets that might otherwise have provided for children's current and future needs. But even when parents approach divorce wisely and reasonably, there are costs, and the whole divorce experience can be shockingly expensive.

Another impact of divorce relates to parents' jobs and careers. A nonworking spouse may need to find a job in order to provide for household expenses. On the other hand, spouses who worked long hours may now need to work less in order to provide direct care to the children when the children are with them. These realities can affect not just parents' day-to-day work schedules but their entire careers as well, as some careers do not accommodate the demands of parenting. Those that require extensive travel or overnight shifts make it very difficult for a parent when there is no spouse at home to provide care for the children. The more co-parents work together on issues like these, the easier they become, but many families have significant, ongoing struggles with them.

Divorce has many other effects on parents as well. In addition to learning how to be single parents during their time with the children, spouses need to become single adults who successfully manage their own lives. One spouse may need to perform household chores—do laundry, fix meals, balance the checkbook, mow the lawn, repair the car—that used to be performed by the other spouse. Spouses must deal with loneliness; while they may have been unhappy in the marriage, at least they were not alone. In addition, they have to face other people's reactions, including those of their own parents, siblings, relatives, and friends. They may also struggle with a sense of failure at the ending of the marriage, even if it was clear that the marriage was no longer working for either spouse. Curiously, despite the prevalence of divorce in our society, there is still some stigma associated with it.

Another challenge for parents involves dealing with the legal system. Relatively few people are ever served with legal papers or faced with the responsibility of hiring a lawyer, and even fewer people have to stand in front of a judge and explain their behavior. When a family goes through a divorce, however, the family enters the judicial system. Beyond all of the other challenges that a divorcing couple might face in dealing with the courts, one of the greatest for parents is how directly and heavily people outside of the family (e.g., attorneys, professionals who are appointed to evaluate or assist the family, and the judge) influence their children's lives. As discussed in Chapter 3, there are family-friendly approaches to divorce that keep the decision making in the hands of the parents. We are dedicated advocates of those approaches, because we firmly believe that parents, when they are willing and capable, are the ideal decision makers when the decisions involve their children.

Throughout the divorce process, parents are faced with the challenge of having too little time to get everything done. It takes time to plan, prepare for, and carry out each step of your divorce, and all of those steps are taking place while you continue to attend to your children's regular needs and the routine tasks of daily life. In addition, your children will need more time from you, as they look to you to patiently guide them through the changes in their lives and in the life of the family. Meanwhile, you cannot and should not put your life on hold, so despite the competing demands, it is essential that you carve out time for your own personal needs. Taking steps to care for yourself is critical if you want to be fully emotionally available to care for your children. All of this takes time, and it may seem that there is simply not enough time to fit in these new tasks. You can, however, find ways to get things done by learning to manage time better so that you can better meet your responsibilities.

The need to develop a working co-parenting relationship is another crucial task faced by parents. Joint parenting has challenges even for intact families, as we each have preferences for how our children should be raised and our own priorities for how to spend time and money. During and after divorce, these challenges increase. There are logistical issues to consider, such as the need to exchange the children and some of their belongings back and forth from one parent to the other, often several times per week. There is also the need to communicate about decisions that must be made about the children, even though the parents may have a hard time speaking to each other civilly about anything.

One of the biggest pitfalls for families of divorce is parental conflict. For many families, conflict lessens after the divorce is finalized, but for others, conflict remains a key issue. It may occur because of strong feelings each parent has about the divorce itself, but it may also result from fundamentally different beliefs the parents hold about how to raise their children. If not kept in check, conflict between co-parents is arguably the most damaging aspect of divorce for children.

Now that we have touched on some of the ways that divorce affects parents, we want to take a close look at how divorce affects children. This information will be useful as you prepare a parenting plan with your co-parent and as you engage in day-to-day parenting and co-parenting after the divorce.

five

How Divorce Affects Your Children

If I had kept my room neater and done my homework, maybe my parents wouldn't have gotten divorced. —Tina, age 7

I wish my parents would still be married so that we'd be a family again. —Sally, age 10

I'm glad that they finally decided to call it quits. It's calmer now that they don't live together, and it's a lot less stressful for me. —Gabe, age 15

These types of comments reflect how children think about divorce. No two children have exactly the same feelings, but most children express similar concerns. Above all, children want their parents to get along, and if their parents can get along with each other, then children wish their parents would stay married. Second, children are stressed by seeing, hearing, or otherwise being exposed to their parents arguing. Third, children prefer not to have their lives complicated. Having to live in two different homes, deal with two sets of rules, and transfer their belongings from place to place are hassles that children dislike.

Beyond these basic themes, children experience a wide range of feelings. They speak of confusion about why things are the way they are, such as why their parents fight so much, or why Dad is so angry at Mom, or why they have to spend half of their time at each house. They share feelings of sadness or loss about how things used to be and how they wish things could be. Some children express guilt about their role in the divorce. Many children report feelings of anger and frustration about how their parents communicate or fail to communicate. They describe feeling nervous or scared about what to expect in both the present and the future.

Part of our goal is to help you become more mindful of how divorce may affect your children's conscious experience and daily life. In addition, we want to help you dig deeper and explore beyond that. Throughout the rest of this chapter, we examine the factors that affect children's *outcomes* as a result of divorce. These outcomes are both short term (i.e., how children function during the months and early years of the divorce) and long term (i.e., how children function when they become adults). To understand these outcomes, we need to go back almost fifty years to trace the early psychological research that was conducted regarding this issue. We will then jump forward to current research that paints a more positive, more accurate, and more helpful picture.

As the divorce rate began to rise dramatically in the United States during the 1960s and 1970s, researchers began to examine the impact of divorce on children. They found that children of divorce were at higher risk for numerous problems compared to children whose parents remained married. Some interpreted this research to suggest that parents should stay together for the sake of the children. We do not believe the answer is that simple; in fact, we believe that many children are better off as a result of their parents' divorce than if their parents had remained married. The early research had problems, or at least limitations. For example, some studies simply compared children whose parents divorced to all other children, including children whose parents were happily married. At a time when divorce was less common and there were greater societal pressures on people to remain married, it is likely that the couples that divorced were different in a variety of ways from couples who remained married. Since the early studies were not comparing apples to apples, the results are of limited value. Recent research has relied on more sophisticated methods to study this issue and has yielded evidence of smaller differences in the outcomes of children whose parents chose to stay married versus children whose parents chose to divorce. This tells us that the earlier conclusions of children being at great risk in divorce were overstated.

Another consideration when looking at research findings is that research identifies group differences, not individual differences. If we say research has shown that children of divorce are more likely to drop out of school early (and it does show that), this does not mean that all children whose parents divorce will drop out early or that a given child will do worse in school because his or her parents divorced. It does not even mean that all studies that looked at this question found the same results. It only means that taken as a whole, in the studies that have examined this issue, there is a statistical difference in group outcomes. Some children perform more poorly in school following their parents' divorce, but some children perform better in school after their parents' divorce. Even though a risk factor may be present, it does not mean that a child will experience the negative outcome associated with it.

Even when looking at the meaningful group differences that do exist, it is our perspective that it is not divorce itself that causes the differences. Rather, it is other factors related to divorce that put children at risk of developing problems. The research suggests that there are also protective factors that decrease risk, mitigating or even eliminating the chance of negative outcomes. The following are risk and protective factors to which parents should attend:

> **Stability.** Divorce is inherently threatening to stability, which is critically important for all children. In addition to adjusting to life with parents living apart from each other, children whose parents divorce often have to deal with multiple other changes, such as leaving their familiar home, moving to a new neighborhood or city,

and perhaps transferring to a new school. In such circumstances, they need to establish new friendships and they may be studying different material. Some things will change; that is unavoidable. Parents should do their best, however, to maximize the stability and continuity in their children's lives. This can be done by ensuring continued access to familiar relationships, remaining in familiar settings (e.g., home, school, daycare, place of worship), and maintaining consistent routines.

Predictability. Uncertainty about when the child will be with each parent and about other key family decisions threatens a child's security. Children need predictable routines if they are to thrive. If parents do not efficiently and effectively manage these decisions, the children's daily lives may be left in limbo. Making major decisions amicably and in a timely manner is one of the best ways to avoid negative fallout on the children. Following through with those joint decisions and maintaining predictable patterns in children's lives to the greatest extent possible is another essential way to minimize problems.

Parental Conflict. This is a critical factor in predicting a child's long-term adjustment following his or her parents' divorce. The more intense the marital conflict, both prior to and after the separation or divorce, and the longer the conflict goes on, the more likely the child will be negatively affected. Placing a child in the middle of the parents' disputes is very damaging. When a parent asks a child to carry a hostile message to the other parent, makes derogatory comments about the other parent in front of the child, or inhibits the child from making positive comments about the other parent, that parent is damaging his or her child. Children need to feel safe about loving and respecting both parents. Parents should do whatever is needed to resolve their conflicts and to minimize the children's exposure to parental conflict.

Parental Availability. Children rely on their parents for emotional support, supervision, advice, instruction, and guidance. The multiple demands of the divorce process often overwhelm parents. They may be preoccupied with their own emotional issues related to the divorce and the need to adjust to a new lifestyle. They may be unable to devote as much attention to their children as they would like. As a result, this can compromise the quality of the children's relationships with one or both parents, and the children must then face these difficult and anxiety-provoking changes in their lives at a time when parental support is least available to them. Parents must be sure that they are emotionally available to their children both during and after the divorce.

Parent-Child Relationship. Having a strong, positive relationship with at least one psychologically healthy parent is important for a child's well-being. Having this type of relationship with both parents is, of course, even better. A parent should recognize that fostering and nurturing a rich and emotionally balanced relationship with his or her children protects them even when the co-parent is not able or willing to provide the same.

Personal Characteristics of the Parents. The parents' personal characteristics constitute another set of risk factors. No parent is perfect, but the more problems a parent has and the more severe these problems are, the greater the risk to the children. This applies to either parent, and is of special concern when both parents exhibit functional problems. The presence of mental health issues or substance abuse problems in a parent can have a negative impact on a child in a number of ways. Such parents may display erratic or poor decision making, inadequately supervise their children, or exhibit destructive behavior toward the child. If a parent is struggling with personal issues, that parent should take steps to receive help. Until these problems are adequately addressed, the parents should consider having the child spend more time with the healthier parent and develop plans to minimize safety risks during the time that the child spends with the less functional parent.

Personal Characteristics of a Child. The children themselves may have risk factors that can compromise their outcomes. For example, a child with preexisting behavioral and emotional problems is at a greater risk of developing more pronounced problems after the divorce. Also, if the parents are not working together to help manage or treat any medical or psychosocial conditions that a child has, those conditions can worsen, especially if the child is living in two homes and one or both parents are unsupportive of the supervision or treatment the child needs. In addition, some children's temperament and personality characteristics make them more vulnerable to the impact of divorce. For example, a child who tends to be sensitive, anxious, or easily frustrated is more likely to react negatively to stressors and unpredictable events. Parents cannot change the temperament of their child, but they can and should ensure that each child's special needs are attended to and, when necessary, that professional support is provided. Notably, children who are doing well prior to a divorce are more likely to continue to do well, and a small percentage of children exhibit a degree of emotional resilience such that they thrive no matter how chaotic their parents' lives become.

Parenting Style. Parenting style is very important. If either parent has inconsistent rules and expectations, uses a harsh and coercive approach to discipline, or engages in erratic or rejecting behaviors toward a child, the child is more likely to develop problems. Ineffective parenting puts children at risk, whereas effective parenting helps to protect children. Effective parenting includes the following:

- Exhibiting warmth and caring
- Providing emotional support
- Having consistent rules, expectations, and consequences
- Adequately monitoring the child's activities and behaviors
- Being actively involved in the child's life
- Encouraging academic skill development
- Providing for the child's basic physical and psychological needs

It is ideal if a child is fortunate enough to get this type of parenting from both parents, but even having just one competent, attentive parent is beneficial. If a parent is limited in his or her ability to parent effectively, that parent should take steps to learn about positive parenting and seek out support to become more effective.

Social Support. Positive sibling relationships help to protect a child, as do positive relationships with grandparents, aunts and uncles, close family friends, and other supportive adults. We believe that any positive social support helps, and the more the better. Parents should foster close, supportive, and actively involved relationships among other family members and reliable family friends.

Beyond the above risk and protective factors, there are other factors that may help or hinder a child's adjustment following the divorce of his or her parents. For example, after a divorce, children typically must learn to cope with living in two places. Living in two homes makes it harder than most adults realize; it means never having all of your stuff in one place at one time. On top of everything else they may be going through, children of divorce may have to do without something that is at the other parent's house, either because the child accidentally forgot it or because he or she is not allowed to take it to the other home. What may seem like a small compromise to a parent may be a big one for the child. These challenges are greatly compounded when the child already struggles with attention problems, inflexibility, or anxiety. By cooperating to ease the sharing and transfer of belongings, parents can lessen the extent to which this is a problem for their child. Finding ways to make this aspect of children's lives easier and more convenient is an important task for both parents during and after a divorce.

Learning to live with new people, including stepparents, stepsiblings, and half siblings, is an enormous challenge even in the best of circumstances. Step relatives can add terrific richness to children's lives and be a wonderful source of support, but adjusting to new family members can also be a source of stress. Parents should carefully consider the timing and methods of introducing new people into the children's lives after divorce. This issue is discussed further in Chapter 11.

To a child, divorce means that family life will forever be different. It is difficult for children to come to terms with the realization that Mom and Dad will no longer be together and the family will no longer be a single unit. This is a huge emotional task for children. Even in the face of all of the conflict and stress, many children fantasize about their parents getting back together. The psychological roller coaster of maintaining this fantasy—wishing for reconciliation, finding hope in it, and then being disappointed when it does not occur—takes a toll on children. Parents can and should help their children understand the changes that are taking place in the family and the permanence of these changes. Many children benefit from the involvement of a counselor or therapist in coming to terms with their new reality.

Also, many families face financial strain during and after a divorce. It is not that children need wealth to be happy; we know that is not true. But if parents are struggling to adjust to a new financial situation, that stress may reduce their ability to parent effectively and to provide the emotional support and guidance that their children will need. A parent may need to go back into the workforce following a divorce, or a parent may need to take on a second job to offset expenses associated with a divorce. Parents need to be, within reason, physically available to their children. When that is unavoidably compromised because of the need to work, parents should develop plans to ensure adequate supervision for the children and focus on the quality of the time they do have with their children, which to a large degree can be even more important than the quantity of time.

We have spoken in general about the negative outcomes that children may experience. More specifically, studies have consistently found that children of divorce are more likely to have emotional problems (e.g., depression, anxiety, lower self-esteem), behavioral issues (e.g., antisocial behaviors, relationship problems, conflict with authority figures, impulsivity), poorer academic performance (e.g., lower achievement test scores, higher dropout rate), and trouble in other areas of their lives (e.g., poorer relationships with their parents, higher adolescent pregnancy rate).

Despite these findings, it is important to remember that the divorce of a child's parents does not predestine that child to a difficult or compromised life. It is true that children whose parents are divorced are more likely as a group to experience emotional and behavioral problems than children whose parents remained married. After a review of the research examining this issue, Dr. Joan Kelly, a prominent researcher in this field, concluded that children whose parents divorced had adjustment problems more than twice as often as children whose parents remained married (25% versus 10%). Another aspect of this data, however, is that between 75% and 80% of the children whose parents divorced fell in the normal range or better on psychological, social, and behavioral measures two to three years after the divorce. In other words, *most children whose parents divorce can ultimately be just as happy, successful, and well-adjusted as children whose parents remain married.*

We believe that the key issue is not whether parents divorce, but the degree to which parents are able to minimize the risk factors and maximize the protective factors discussed above. By taking note of these factors, and by taking decisive and unified action based on them, parents can have enormous influence over their children's ultimate outcomes. This is why mindful co-parenting is so essential.

six

Selecting Your Co-parenting Approach

Bruce and Emily seemed to have a reasonably happy marriage. They both felt close to their two daughters and there wasn't a lot of conflict or tension in their home. But two years ago, things started to go downhill. Emily became critical of Bruce's time spent playing poker at a local casino, and she became more and more concerned that his losses were threatening their long-term financial plans. Bruce, in turn, started to feel that Emily was treating him like a child, that she was constantly monitoring him, and that all she really cared about was how much money they had in their bank account. The irritation on both sides turned into sarcastic comments back and forth. Eventually they found that they didn't trust each other anymore and didn't like being around each other. One night, during a heated argument, their eight-year-old daughter came to them crying and said, "Why do you have to hate each other?" Bruce took their daughter back to her bed without being able to think of an answer for her and then returned to Emily. At that moment, they realized that their conflict had crossed a line, as it was now clearly harming their child. The next day they made arrangements to see a marriage therapist. They continued seeing the therapist for four months, and while some things got better, they ended up making the decision to end their marriage. Bruce and Emily were getting divorced. There were many questions to answer, but one of the most important was this: What kind of co-parenting relationship were they going to have after the divorce?

There are a variety of ways that co-parents can relate to one another after a divorce. Some parents find that they can be supportive friends. Others find that they can be pleasant and cooperative, but with some emotional distance. Still others find that they cannot tolerate interaction, but they can provide good parenting when the children are with them, and they can allow the other parent to do the same. There are many ways to make co-parenting work, which is fortunate because not every pair of co-parents can do it the same way.

Postdivorce co-parenting relationships can be viewed as falling along a broad continuum in terms of their degree of conflict. Some may have almost no conflict while others may have vast amounts. For the purpose of simplifying our discussion about parenting plans, we will identify three major categories along this continuum: low, moderate-to-high, and severe. Your postdivorce relationship may fall squarely in one of these categories or it may fall in between two of them, but most co-parents are able to identify which category is closest to their own experience.

Low Conflict

Co-parenting relationships with low conflict are those in which the parents are able to drop their guard, to communicate honestly, and to readily adjust to accommodate reasonable requests from each other. The interactions may or may not be warm and friendly, but at the very least, for the vast majority of the time, the interactions are at least civil and cordial. The parents in this category view the important undertaking of raising their children as a joint effort. There may be brief periods of more pronounced conflict, but these parents are able to rationally approach that conflict and find ways to resolve it or contain it.

Moderate-to-High Conflict

Co-parents who experience moderate-to-high conflict have a less predictable relationship. They may go long periods of time operating with moderate conflict only to find that, for reasons they do not fully understand, they suddenly experience weeks or months of higher conflict. What tends to be consistent is that negative emotions arise easily and the parents are frequently locked in a power struggle. This impairs their communication, and one or both parents are less willing to accommodate requests. There is typically some degree of anger and hostility in these relationships, at least on the part of one of the parents.

Severe Conflict

Finally, there are co-parents with such severe conflict that they fall at the far end of the spectrum. Their relationships are characterized by the consistent presence of open hostility and a desire of one or both parents either to completely ignore or to antagonize the other. At least one of the parents has a corrosive effect on the other. Even when they appear to be tolerating one another, there is usually a sense of dread that bad things might happen soon.

These three categories of conflict in a co-parenting relationship are depicted here:

Parents should choose a co-parenting approach that aligns with the level of conflict that exists in their relationship. By doing so, they can structure their interactions so that the conflict is better managed and does not escalate. The goal of this is protect the children; the less that children experience the co-parenting conflict, the better off they will be. Parents have a responsibility to protect their children from being placed in the middle of their disputes and a duty to shield them from exposure to any significant tension or hostility that might arise between the parents.

The co-parenting approaches that align with the co-parenting levels of conflict are the following:

In this diagram, the first approach, *cooperative co-parenting*, is the approach that best fits for co-parents with low-conflict relationships. The second approach, *parallel co-parenting*, is the better match for relationships with moderate-to-high conflict, while *encapsulated co-parenting* is the right match for relationships with severe conflict. We will review each of these approaches in detail and explain when they fit, why they fit, and how you can use them to guide you toward a more functional co-parenting interaction that is suited to your circumstances.

Cooperative Co-parenting

In cooperative co-parenting, each parent communicates regularly and easily with the other parent. The ability to communicate clearly and without hostility defines a low conflict co-parenting relationship and is a hallmark of this approach. Another hallmark is each parent's ability and willingness to bend when the other parent makes a reasonable request. For example, if Parent A asks Parent B to allow the children to stay late at his or her house on Saturday so that they can watch a movie marathon, Parent B is very likely to agree, even if it creates some inconvenience, as long as there are no major concerns about any negative impact the arrangement might have on the children. Likewise, if Parent B wishes to plan a longer period of travel with the children during summer break than the parenting plan indicates, Parent A is likely to make every effort to accommodate the request.

In cooperative co-parenting, children are allowed reasonable freedom to adjust their schedules and to travel between the homes to pick up their sports equipment, school items, or favorite articles of clothing. When a dispute arises, parents resolve it through calm discussion and avoid stonewalling or verbal attacks, thereby insulating the children from their disagreements. Parents who use cooperative co-parenting are also good at respecting boundaries and following rules, so they respect each other's time with the children and stay within the lines when an agreement is reached.

There are obvious advantages to cooperative co-parenting over other approaches. The lack of tension creates a more normal family environment for children. In addition, the high level of flexibility makes it easier to accommodate the needs of both the children and their parents. Finally, this approach is more efficient, with little or no time, energy, or money wasted on conflict. Parents work together as a team, helping each other in the shared life project of raising their children to adulthood.

Parallel Co-parenting

The second co-parenting approach is parallel co-parenting, which is geared toward co-parents who fall in the moderate-to-high conflict category. Because parents in this category are not able to sustain a sufficiently positive and coordinated relationship to make the cooperative approach work, it is essential that they have a way to navigate their conflicts with the least amount of stress and strain between them. Asking parents with greater conflict to use a cooperative co-parenting method is likely to do more harm than good, so we strongly recommend that parents with a moderate-to-high level of conflict consider a parallel co-parenting approach. This is also a preferable method for parents with poorer boundaries, dysfunctional communication, or inflexibility.

With parallel co-parenting, co-parents interact on a limited and controlled basis. Communication takes place only when it is needed, and it typically occurs via email or text to avoid the conflicts that arise in spoken exchanges. Parents make joint decisions only for major decisions, such as which school the children will attend or whether a child will have a serious medical procedure. Each parent handles daily life with the children separately, with minimal interaction between one another. They are still required to inform each other when school reports are received or when the children have medical appointments, but the communication is limited to notification, with little or no discussion taking place. When using a parallel co-parenting approach, parents follow the timesharing schedule[4] with few alterations, and they learn to make accommodations within their own lives to deal with scheduling challenges without involving each other. For example, if a father has a work conflict that prevents him from picking up his son from soccer practice, he might have his sister or a close family friend pick up the child rather than arranging for the mother to step in.

In some ways, one might think of parallel co-parenting as two single parents sharing responsibility for a child, with interaction only in regard to major decisions. Another way to describe this approach is to imagine the parallel rails of a railroad track. Picture the children moving down one rail of a railroad track when with one parent and down the other rail when with the other parent. Either way, they are moving in the same direction toward the same destination, but each rail is independent of the other. Hopefully, the parents are both working in the same direction in terms of fostering their children's health and well-being, their academic progress, and their social and emotional development, but the way that they go about achieving those ends may differ from one another.

While parallel co-parenting may not be the ideal way to raise children, it is much better than engaging in ongoing conflict. By reducing interaction, there are fewer opportunities for friction between parents, and less friction means less stress for everyone. Children do not have

---

4 The term *timesharing schedule* refers to the specific schedule that defines the days and times that the children are with each parent. Timesharing issues are discussed at length in Chapter 8.

to see their parents argue, nor do they have to overhear confrontational phone conversations. They also avoid the negative effects of being around a parent who just had an angry interaction with the other parent and may be stewing about it. All of these factors help to protect the children from exposure to hostility between their parents. Finally, parallel co-parenting is helpful to some parents as they move on with their own lives, as it allows each parent to live with less intrusion from the other parent.

Encapsulated Co-parenting

When the parenting conflict is severe, or there is a history of angry outbursts or threats of violence, we recommend a third approach to co-parenting that we call encapsulated co-parenting. Some divorce professionals see this approach as being an extension of parallel co-parenting, but we think that there are enough unique aspects to encapsulated co-parenting that it is best explained and understood as its own distinct approach. The encapsulated approach takes the chaos and volatility of severe conflict and contains it so that it does not escalate, thereby minimizing the fallout on the children. This approach applies specific guidelines to buffer the children from parental conflict and to protect the parents themselves from explosive interactions. The following types of provisions are generally recommended:

- The co-parents rigidly follow the timesharing schedule and make special requests only in the presence of a third party, such as a parenting coordinator or a family therapist.
- Both parents do not attend any special events without a specific, detailed arrangement that is worked out in advance to assure that no negative interaction will occur. When an arrangement cannot be made that allows both parents to attend the same event in a safe

manner, then one parent must miss that event. While disappointing to that parent, and possibly to a child as well, some co-parenting relationships require this restriction in order to protect the children.

- Parents use phone communication (calls or texts) for emergencies only.

- Email communication is monitored by a professional and/or is conducted via a website that is designed to help high-conflict parents communicate. Many of these sites provide a calendar for communicating about children's activities, allowing both parents to know what is going on in the lives of their children without requiring direct communication between the parents.

There are significant downsides to encapsulated co-parenting. One downside is that it creates a family environment that may feel polarized and unnatural. Another is that there is minimal flexibility in adjusting schedules and other matters, and that can feel overly restrictive to the children. While these downsides are unfortunate, an encapsulated approach is a necessary choice for families in which the co-parenting conflict is severe.

Hybrid Approaches

There are hybrid approaches that combine elements of the three co-parenting approaches discussed above. For example, Annie and George are co-parents who use a parallel co-parenting approach for the most part, but they find that they are able to successfully incorporate some aspects of a cooperative approach. They will often accommodate each other when it comes to trading days in the timesharing schedule, and they are generally open to arranging for George to provide childcare while Annie works. In a pure parallel approach, these activities would not typically occur. On the other hand, Charles and

Samantha, who use a cooperative co-parenting approach in general, have found the need to apply a parallel approach to certain aspects of their co-parenting. When their communication began to slip into bickering, they agreed to restrict themselves to emails and texts. They also decided to follow a rule that any requests for trading parenting time must be made at least two weeks in advance. These are examples of how hybrid approaches can allow for the tailoring of the co-parenting approach to the needs of a particular family.

ಎಲ್

The three primary approaches can be easily distinguished by exploring how each approach might deal with the same set of circumstances. For example, when the physical exchange of the children cannot be done at school, an alternative solution needs to be found. With cooperative co-parenting, the exchange is likely to take place at one of the parent's homes. With parallel co-parenting, it may need to take place at a neutral site or with a scripted arrangement at one of the homes, such as having the parent who is picking up the children wait in the car and having the children walk out to the car while the parent in the house stays inside. With encapsulated co-parenting, the exchange may need to involve a third party, with either a mutually trusted family member transporting the children between parents, or a trained professional overseeing the exchange with both parents present. The exchange may even need to occur at a law enforcement facility, such as a sheriff's office or police station.

Without a doubt, children whose parents fail to embrace an appropriate approach will suffer as a result. Parents should identify a co-parenting approach that takes into account their level of conflict, and then apply that approach conscientiously and consistently. Which approach is right for your family? This question is important because it gets to the heart of mindful co-parenting. Remember, mindful co-parenting is about paying attention on an ongoing basis to what your children need and what works for your family. This means that *the approach that is right for your family is the one that fits your unique family circumstances.*

With that in mind, we believe that cooperative co-parenting is preferable if you and your co-parent have a low-conflict relationship and if you mutually agree to use that approach. The choice hinges on your ability to communicate effectively with each other and to maintain a low level of conflict. If you can do both of these things consistently, then it is worth trying a cooperative approach. If, however, you cannot do these things consistently, then a parallel co-parenting approach is more likely to work for you. If you cannot even tolerate being in the same room together without hurling insults or glaring at each other with animosity, then an encapsulated approach is the one you need.

Your selection of a co-parenting approach is not set in stone. You always have the option of jointly deciding to shift from one approach to the other if the quality of your co-parenting relationship changes. If you have used a parallel co-parenting approach and you both feel that you can now work cooperatively, then an adjustment might be in order. Likewise, if you have tried cooperative co-parenting but you are now finding that you are experiencing greater conflict, you can move to a more structured, parallel co-parenting approach. There is one caveat to this, however: The co-parenting approach you choose influences the formal, written parenting plan that you develop. The reason for this is that a parenting plan based on cooperative co-parenting will allow, or even require, more interaction between parents than one based on parallel or encapsulated co-parenting. When in doubt, parents should write a parenting plan that is at least somewhat restrictive (requiring less communication, less interaction, and less flexibility). As we will discuss in the next chapter, the written plan serves as a safety net, and a tight net is safer than a loose one. That said, the written plan should not constrain you from cooperating if a mutually cooperative spirit is truly present.

Keep in mind that a cooperative co-parenting approach requires that *both* parents are able and willing to communicate and to be flexible.

If either parent is unable to adhere to these requirements, then the other parent cannot carry the less-able or less-willing parent through. They say, "It takes two to tango," and that is certainly the case when it comes to cooperative co-parenting. Likewise, a parallel co-parenting approach will not work when one parent is able to restrain himself from lashing out but the other parent is not. A family such as this requires an encapsulated approach.

At the start of this chapter, we wrote about Bruce and Emily. At the time of their divorce, they each felt quite hurt:

> When Emily learned that Bruce had put them $160,000 into debt with his gambling, and when, during one hearing in their divorce process, Emily's attorney referred to Bruce as "a pitiful loser" (a label that Emily had used in one of her angry emails to Bruce), the hurt compounded. As a result of the strong distrust on both sides and the fact that neither of them could tolerate much communication, Bruce and Emily realized that they needed to start with a parallel co-parenting approach. They arranged for their parenting plan to be written accordingly, and they both followed that approach for the first year and a half after their divorce was finalized. By that time, their anger had softened a good deal and some healing had taken place. They both wanted to have a more cooperative co-parenting relationship for the benefit of their daughters and were ready to try. In the end, Bruce and Emily were able to accomplish that goal, and the whole family is now reaping the rewards.

seven

The Parenting Plan: Decision Making

Good co-parenting requires a good parenting plan. The parenting plan serves several important functions. It is, first and foremost, a blueprint for your co-parenting relationship, as it describes how you and your co-parent will work together on behalf of your children. The parenting plan also serves as a figurative safety net for when disputes arise that you and your co-parent are otherwise unable to resolve. Some families discover that they can work very cooperatively and do not have to rely on their formal plan over time. Having a good plan to guide the process is essential, however, and it is an invaluable safeguard for times of conflict. For these reasons, the parenting plan has earned its place as a fundamental, divorce-related, legal document.

The process of developing the parenting plan helps you to organize your thinking about co-parenting. As a starting point, it leads you to focus on the co-parenting approach (cooperative, parallel, or encapsulated) that is right for your family. Keeping that approach in mind helps you to design a plan that predicts problems and offers ways to avoid them. Organizing your thinking also means making a number of specific decisions in a proactive manner. A very basic example is found in the way that co-parents alternate a holiday by year, with one parent having the children at his or her home for Thanksgiving in even-numbered years and the other having the children in his or her home in odd-numbered years. By arranging this treatment of the holiday in advance, the parents prevent any disputes that might arise later about where the children will be for Thanksgiving dinner. Although it may feel burdensome to address multiple time frames and other seemingly minor items in advance, it is a wise investment of time and effort in the long run. By dealing with these issues while developing their parenting plan, parents ensure that they will not have to negotiate these points later in the midst of a dispute. This proactive attention to detail can also prevent costly, subsequent litigation and provide a sense of closure on the primary co-parenting negotiations.

Defining how the parents will structure their co-parenting relationship, and doing so in a formal document, can actually help improve the quality of life for the parents. It offers them some certainty to rely on, which in turn allows them to move forward more easily in their individual lives. The true goal of a parenting plan, however, is to create the best possible plan for the children.

No two families are exactly alike, so cookie-cutter parenting plans are not appropriate. Each family needs to develop its own unique plan that takes into account the particular needs and circumstances of each child and both parents. If parents are cooperating, they can be as creative as they wish in addressing the needs of their children. There are general principles, however, that apply to virtually all families, and we will address many of these in this chapter and the two that follow. There are also two fundamental elements that must be included in *all* parenting plans: One is timesharing, which we will cover in Chapter 8, and the other is decision making. The remainder of this chapter is devoted to decision making and how it should be addressed in a parenting plan.

Decision making focuses on which types of decisions a parent can make unilaterally and which types require both parents to agree. In general, on a day-to-day basis, each parent independently makes routine decisions when the children are in that parent's care. Examples of routine decisions include bedtimes, meal selection, clothing options, television and other electronic devices, play date schedules, and homework supervision. It is ideal when parents can communicate about such issues and provide consistency between the two homes, but when this fails, the parent caring for the children at that time makes the decisions. If there are any limitations on routine decision making, these should be clearly spelled out in the parenting plan.

Another type of decision a parent makes unilaterally involves emergencies. Each parent should have full authority to make emergency decisions, especially emergency medical care. The rationale for this is obvious: There may not be time to allow for communication and discussion between two parents in a truly emergent situation. If one parent has sole responsibility for the decision making regarding all medical care (a possibility that we will address below), then it is imperative that the parenting plan state that the other parent may respond to medical emergencies when the child is in his or her care. If the other parent is not allowed to do so, then the plan *must* delineate how such situations are to be handled.

Both routine and emergency decisions are fairly easy to describe in the parenting plan, as they usually fall to the parent who has the children at that time. A more significant aspect of decision making involves major decisions. The following are some of the major decisions that most parents address in their children's parenting plan:

- **Health care:** Medical, dental, optic, orthodontic, psychological, psychiatric, counseling, and similar services
- **Education and day care/aftercare:** Selection of a school, day care programs for younger children, and aftercare programs for elementary and middle-school students
- **Religion:** Attendance at a place of worship, formal religious training, and participation in a baptism, christening, bar mitzvah, or similar ceremony
- **Extracurricular activities:** Sports, scouting, music lessons, clubs, and summer camps

In addition, some families identify other major decisions to incorporate into the parenting plan. These might include whether to allow children to attend out-of-town field trips or trips with people other than their parents and when to allow them to begin working as a babysitter or to obtain a driving permit. We have each worked with families that chose to include some very specific decisions, such as whether to allow children and teenagers to get ear piercings or tattoos or to participate in high-risk activities such as bungee jumping or skydiving. As with other areas of the parenting plan, parents must consider how they hope to raise their children over many years. Some of the language included in the plan might relate to matters that may not happen anytime soon, especially if the children are still infants or toddlers. When writing a parenting plan involving a three-year-old, it may be hard to think about how you will feel about decisions affecting your child's teenage years, but now is the time to construct the best plan that you can by anticipating what will matter to you and to your children in the future. This does not necessarily mean you should make a written commitment as to what your future decision will be, but that you should at least specify how you and your co-parent will come to that decision in the future. This sometimes involves a combination of a specific decision and a process for overriding that decision, e.g., the child may not have a tattoo prior to the age of eighteen unless both parents agree.

There are several ways to define which major decisions a parent can make unilaterally and which ones require both parents to agree. The two primary approaches are *shared decision making* and *sole decision making*. In addition to these, there are two variations, one of which is referred to as *divided decision making* and the other as *shared decision making with ultimate decision making authority*. We address each of these four options in detail below.

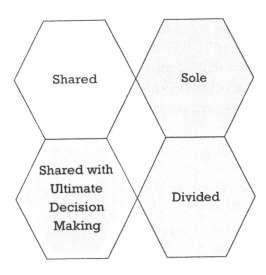

Shared Decision Making

Unless there is a good reason not to do so, most parents share authority for making major decisions about their children. There are a number of advantages to this. *Shared decision making* helps to keep both parents actively involved in the lives of their children. It allows for parents to consider each other's perspective and to weigh all the pros and cons, which in turn helps guide them to more thoroughly considered decisions. Sharing decisions also provides a form of checks and balances to prevent either parent from making extreme choices on core matters that might negatively affect the children.

There are downsides to shared decision making, however, as parents with a moderate-to-high level of conflict often find that conversations about decisions can escalate into arguments and heightened hostility. In some cases, these arguments take an even more drastic turn and spur new litigation. It is for these reasons that shared decision making is contraindicated for parents with severe conflict, i.e., those who require an encapsulated co-parenting approach. Even some parents who utilize a parallel co-parenting approach will find shared decision making problematic. As difficult as settling disagreements about parenting can be for married parents who get along well, it is all the more difficult for a divorced couple with a history of conflict. Sometimes one parent will use shared decision making as a weapon to frustrate the other parent. This can leave the children living in a state of limbo while parents battle nonstop over basic decisions. There are, however, ways in which this can be addressed.

If parents choose to have shared decision making, they should state how they will handle any situations in which they are unable to reach consensus about a major decision. One way to address this is to stipulate that when parents are unable to agree, they will engage a professional to help them discuss their difference so that they can reach a mutual, final decision. Another option is to have this professional serve as an arbitrator (i.e., decision maker) for specific, limited decisions. (In some states, professionals can be empowered by the court to make decisions for parents when the parents are at an impasse.) In our opinion, this should always be a last resort, as we feel strongly that it is best for parents to jointly make decisions for their own children. A third option would be to specify that one or both parents are empowered to make certain decisions when consensus is not reached (see the discussion on Shared Decision Making with Ultimate Decision Making Authority below).

Sole Decision Making

One alternative to shared decision making is *sole decision making*. In sole decision making, one parent is fully empowered to make some or all major decisions, such as those that relate to education, healthcare, or religion, without the input of the other parent. There is no requirement or expectation that the parents will try to work together to agree on a decision. If one parent has a condition that impairs his judgment and compromises his ability to make good choices, then sole decision making for the other parent may be necessary.

Professionals generally agree that sole decision making should be selected only when there is clear evidence that it is necessary to protect the interests of the children. Leaving one parent out of the process of making major decisions can disenfranchise that parent and may be seen as infringing on that parent's rights, so it should be the course chosen only when other options are not appropriate.

Divided Decision Making

Another option is *divided decision making*. Divided decision making separates out the major types of decisions (e.g., health care, education, extracurricular activities, and religion) and allows one or both parents to have sole decision making for one or more specific areas. For example, the parents might have shared decision making for most major decisions involving the children, but the mother could be granted the right to make any and all decisions about a particular matter, such as extracurricular activities. While the parents must reach a consensus for all other major decisions, the mother would make the decisions related to extracurricular activities and it would be up to her to determine whether she wished to seek input from the father. Regardless of the mother's decision, however, she would be required to communicate the decision to the father once the decision is made. Alternatively both parents might have areas for which he or she unilaterally makes the decisions. For example, the father may have sole decision making for the children's education and the mother may have sole decision making for the children's religious upbringing. This might be done because the parent being granted sole decision making authority has better expertise in a particular field. For example, if the father or the mother is a dentist, the parents may decide that this parent is more capable of making decisions about the children's dental care.

Divided decision making might also be used when both parents are capable of making good choices, but they recognize that they reflexively disagree with one another and become more rigid and inflexible the longer they debate an issue. As a result, it is determined that they simply cannot reach agreements together, and the better option is for their decision making to be divided right from the start.

The problem with divided decision making, however, is that it blocks out one parent or the other from having the right to negotiate to reach an agreement. For this reason, this approach is not frequently used.

Shared Decision Making with Ultimate Decision Making Authority

Parents who value shared decision making, but who are ineffective at making decisions together, need to have a way to protect their children from the resulting gridlock. An option for these parents is *shared decision making with ultimate decision making authority.* Ultimate decision making authority recognizes that when parents are unable to resolve certain disputes jointly, one parent must be allowed to make that decision on behalf of the children. This approach requires that the parents confer and attempt to reach agreement on any major decisions concerning the children. This is expected to be a genuine, good faith effort toward working things out together. If the parents, despite making a concerted effort, are unable to reach an agreement, then one parent is empowered with the authority to make the final decision.

Ultimate decision making authority may be granted to one parent for one or more major decisions, or it may be granted to one parent for certain major decisions and to the other parent for other major decisions. In many cases, this authority is provided to a parent for just a single type of decision; for example, the mother might have the final say regarding educational matters and the father might have the final say regarding health-care matters. The remainder of the major decisions are shared between parents without either parent having the final say for those decisions.

Ultimate decision making authority has some of the attributes of shared, sole, and divided decision making. It requires the parents to first attempt to reach a consensus on all major decisions. It allows, however, for one parent to make a unilateral decision when consensus is not reached. And finally, it does not have to be all-or-none, but instead it can be divided. One parent can have final authority for one or more areas while the other parent has authority over different areas. For all of these reasons, this decision-making approach has become increasingly prevalent over recent years.

eight

The Parenting Plan: Timesharing

Most parents value time with their children above all else. It is for this reason that timesharing is such a significant and weighty portion of the parenting plan for all families. We consider dividing the limited days of the children's lives to be a very serious task.

There are many facets to timesharing. One of these is the amount of time the children spend with each parent, which we refer to as the *allocation* of parenting time. Another of these is the *timesharing schedule*, which spells out which specific days and hours the children will spend with each parent. The timesharing schedule includes rules for how to divide school breaks and holidays, how to deal with the children's birthdays, and how to arrange vacation times so each parent can have blocks of time to travel with the children. Yet another facet of timesharing involves how the children are exchanged from the care of one parent to the other. In the course of this chapter, we will explore each of these aspects of timesharing.

At a minimum, the timesharing arrangements must address the following:

- How much time is best for the children to spend with each parent?
- On which days of the week will the children be with each parent?

- At what time of day will the children go from one parent to the other?
- What is the longest time each child should be away from either parent?
- How many transitions between parents are preferable?
- How will exchanges be handled?

Determining the Allocation of Parenting Time

We believe that any discussion of time allocation should begin with a basic understanding about the primacy of parents as caregivers to their children. When both parents are available and capable of parenting effectively, the parents should be their children's primary care providers. This does not mean that grandparents, nannies, or day care services should not be utilized, but simply that the parents should be the direct providers of care whenever that is possible and reasonable.[5]

How much time should a child be with each parent? Assuming that there are two emotionally healthy, competent parents, it is ideal if each parent has a substantial amount of time to engage in normal routines with the children, such as getting them ready for bed, overseeing homework, and preparing them for school. The number of hours and days that children spend with each parent will vary from family to family; as with parenting plans in general, one size does not fit all. Without knowing a great deal about your family, we cannot tell you what is best for your children. There are, however, a number of factors for parents to consider, ten of which are listed below.

1. *Age and Maturity*

As children grow, they progress through several developmental stages, each of which brings new capabilities and new needs. Two factors that relate to a child's developmental stage are age and level of maturity, and these factors have important implications for timesharing. For example,

---

5 Every rule has exceptions, and there are some cases in which a parent may not be the best choice. For example, if there are valid concerns about the fitness of either parent, then measures must be taken to ensure that the children are safe and well cared for.

if parents agree on the benefits of breastfeeding an infant beyond the early months, they may arrange to have the baby spend the vast majority of his or her first year with the mother. On the other hand, a four-year-old may be able to spend an equal amount of time with each parent. As the child grows and matures there are other considerations. For example, that four-year-old may need to see each parent at least every few days, as longer separations from either parent may cause distress, while most fifteen-year-olds can handle longer separations.

Many parents believe that young children need more time with their mothers during what are often called *the tender years*. This perspective is not consistently supported by research, but there is also no evidence that younger children are harmed by having a larger percentage of time with a competent, nurturing mother as long as they continue to develop a meaningful relationship with their father. Recent studies have highlighted the critical contribution of paternal involvement, so we now better recognize that *both* parents play important roles in raising children. A family may choose to allow more parenting time with Mom than with Dad, but if this is done in a way that compromises the father-child relationship, then there may be a net loss for the child.

Some researchers advise against regular overnights in more than one home for very young children, especially those age three and below. They contend that doing so needlessly challenges a child. Other researchers, however, posit that competent parents who are actively involved in their children's lives can and should have the children for overnights; they argue that having overnights in both homes fosters the child's attachment to each parent and supports an engaged relationship of each parent with the child. Research has not yet concluded which perspective is more correct. At the present time, family circumstances and the parents' preferences must guide this timesharing decision.

2. *Special Needs*

Parents must take into account any special needs their child may have when determining the amount of time the child spends with each parent.

For example, if a child has an anxiety disorder, an attention deficit, or a behavioral problem, that child may require greater levels of structure and stability. The parents may choose to forgo some of the benefits of having each parent be highly involved in order to provide the additional stability that comes from one parent taking a larger role, or to allow one parent's home to serve as a base for the child's daily routine. Likewise, if a child has a complex physical illness, such as diabetes or cerebral palsy, one parent may be better suited to handling the regimens associated with managing or treating the condition. These are complex decisions for parents that often require one or both parents to make considerable sacrifices.

3. *Child's Relationship to Each Parent*

For any number of different reasons, a child may be closer to one parent or the other, or one parent may have an easier time parenting one or more of the children. It is reasonable to consider this factor in timesharing and to remain open to the need to modify a timesharing schedule at any time if the parent-child relationship changes in meaningful ways. A seven-year-old who is much more attached to his mother may have a stronger relationship with his father when he reaches age twelve, and the timesharing schedule should accommodate this possibility.

4. *Parenting Capacity and Involvement*

Some parents have better parenting skills than others and are more focused on their children's overall needs. Such parents may naturally provide a warm, nurturing environment and be more available to the children in both practical and emotional ways. They may be more adept at monitoring the children and setting limits constructively and consistently. When this is the case, it makes sense for the children to spend more time with that parent, but this does not imply that children should spend very little time with the less capable parent. That parent may have a lot to learn, but could, after the divorce, develop the skills to be an exceptional parent. And even if that parent continues to be less competent in some ways, he or she may have other strengths that will serve the children. Only in extreme cases should this imbalance substantially restrict the time that the children spend with the less-skilled parent. One such extreme case might be a parent's inability to provide adequate supervision, which could expose the children to an unsafe environment or to distinctly negative influences; another would be a parent's untreated substance abuse problem or an unmanaged mental illness.

5. *Historical Level of Involvement*

Using a parent's historical level of involvement in the children's daily lives as the basis for determining the allocation of parenting time is controversial. Some theorists have proposed that this should be the primary consideration. Their reasoning is that it would be a simple way for courts to determine a timesharing arrangement and thus might discourage parents from engaging in lengthy litigation. This might be beneficial, but many couples have based their levels of involvement in child rearing on teamwork and a division of responsibilities. When they divorce, maintaining that arrangement might no longer be realistic or desirable for one or both of them. More importantly, maintaining the status quo might not be in the best interest of the children.

For example, if the mother earned the bulk of the income while the marriage was intact, the parents might have agreed that the father would stay home and provide the majority of the care to the children. The family routine might have been that Mom came home in time to have dinner with the family each night—a dinner that Dad prepared. After dinner, Mom spent an hour exercising, checking personal email, and unwinding while Dad supervised the children and cleaned up. About an hour before bedtime, Mom helped the children with their homework and spent some time playing with them. The parents equally shared bath time and getting the children ready for bed. In this case, Dad is doing most of the child care. But if these parents divorced, Dad might have to go back to work. Mom might say, "I never wanted to work so much; we just needed the money, and I wanted to enable the children to be home with one of us. I sacrificed for the common good, but I want to and can share equally in the parenting time after the divorce." If this couple based their timesharing plan on their individual historical involvement, the children would spend eighty percent of their overnights with their father, significantly reducing their exposure to their mother after the divorce and limiting the positive things she could contribute to their upbringing.

Although we do not believe that the historical level of involvement of each parent should be the primary consideration for all families, the continuity of care of children *is* important. If children are used to spending the majority of their time with one parent, and that parent has developed consistent routines with them, this should be weighed into the decision of how much time the children spend with each parent in the future. Also, a parent who has spent much more time with the children may have honed his or her parenting skills as a result of this additional time and thus become a more competent parent. At the very least, the competence of this parent may have been well demonstrated, whereas the ability of the other parent to sustain those consistent routines is an unknown. When both parents are deemed to be adequately competent, gradually increasing the amount of parenting time of a previously less-involved parent reduces the level of disruption and allows the children to adjust to this incrementally. It may also allow that parent to learn how to establish and maintain consistent routines with the children prior to the children spending larger amounts of time with that parent.

6. *Adequacy, Safety, Stability, and Continuity of the Homes*

We have repeatedly referred to the advantages of having two, well-adjusted parents who are fully involved in the care of the children. These advantages rely on the assumption that both homes are adequate, safe, and stable, and offer continuity.

A home's adequacy refers to its basic features and infrastructure: a room for the children to sleep in and to maintain their belongings, appropriate utilities (plumbing, electricity, heat), and access to public services or schools. Safety refers both to the absence of known dangers in the home, such as lead paint, unsecured weapons, and dangerous chemicals, as well as to reasonable evidence that the neighborhood is safe for children. Stability refers to the children's confidence that their parent will meet all major adult responsibilities: The parent will always provide appropriate food and clothing, determine who will be present in the home, decide who is responsible for which activities, and maintain a reasonable consistency in routines. Continuity refers to a committed effort to avoid having the children move repeatedly from one residence to the next, which sometimes occurs when a co-parent and the children must reside in a series of short-term rental apartments.

If one co-parent's home cannot meet all of these requirements, then the parents must try to work out a plan that accounts for these deficiencies. In the meantime, until a suitable venue can be arranged, having the children overnight may not be reasonable for that co-parent. Daytime activities at an appropriate location outside of the home may need to be used on a temporary basis to provide a way for that parent to spend time with the children while they live at the other parent's home.

7. Familiar Home, School, and Neighborhood

Divorce is a time of tumultuous change in a child's life. Although this is unavoidable, parents are well-advised to do all they can to minimize it. If children can remain in the marital home while they are adjusting to the new family structure, they may take some comfort from the familiarity of that home. This does not mean they need to be in the marital home more than half of the time, but it is easier to adjust to one new home than to adjust to two new homes, especially at the same time. Staying in the same school, whenever possible, is also highly desirable, as is remaining in the same neighborhood or near the children's friends. For many families, this may not be financially possible, so the parents must focus on maintaining as much consistency and familiarity as they can for their children.

8. Locations of the Homes

The location of the parents' homes relative to one another is an important factor to consider. Transporting the children from one home to the other, or from each home to and from school, can be easy or difficult depending on how far the parents live from one another and from the schools. If the parents live far away from one another or far away from the schools, the number of transitions needs to be limited so that their children do not spend inordinate amounts of time en route. Distance between homes can limit the options for timesharing schedules. A schedule that has the children with each parent for two consecutive weekdays and alternating weekends can work well if both parents live within twenty minutes of the children's schools, but it will not work well if one parent lives in a different city that is three hours away. Even if both parents live in the same city, if one is a one-hour drive from the school, the parents need to evaluate whether two hours of commuting in a day is in the best interests of the child. The ideal situation is when parents live in the same part of the same city or town as one another; this allows the children to have easy access to their schools and neighborhood friends, even if the parents don't live in the same neighborhood. Many divorcing or divorced parents prefer not to have too much proximity, so it is not uncommon for the ex-spouses to select different parts of town in which to reside as a way of creating some independence and emotional space. While this is understandable, it is essential that they consider the impact on the children. Beyond its effect on access to schools and neighborhood friends, a large distance between homes can create problems for participation in extracurricular activities, especially sports that require a child to attend multiple practices and games each week. When parents live far from one another, there can be a tug-of-war over where their child will attend gymnastics classes or which soccer league their child will join. Distance between homes also breeds greater conflict over the selection of schools, and such conflicts can result in impasses that require court intervention.

9. Support of the Other Parent's Relationship with the Children

A pivotal aspect of the co-parenting relationship is how well each parent supports the children's relationships with the other parent. For example, if Parent A consistently makes negative comments about Parent B, or does other things to undermine the children's feelings toward that parent, then it may not be best for the children to spend a lot of time with Parent A. Whether Parent A realizes it or not, his or her attitude toward Parent B can undermine the relationships the children have with *both* parents.

Whether this behavior is intentional or unintentional—reflecting, perhaps, the hurt and anger that Parent A experienced as a result of the divorce—a helpful parenting plan might limit the time the children are around that parent until he or she has participated in therapy to work through these issues and is able to co-parent more positively. In such cases, however, history shows that the offending parent is almost always resistant to agreeing to such limitations. Imposing such a timesharing requirement invariably requires a court order.

10. Children's Preferences

Children should never be made to feel that they are being asked to choose between their parents. We strongly recommend letting children know that the allocation of parenting time is an adult decision made jointly by the parents, or sometimes by a judge. However, while children should not be burdened by such weighty decisions or made to worry about the feelings of one or both parents, the older the child is, the more that child's preferences should be considered. Listening to what the child wants does not mean that parents should make the decision about timesharing based solely on that; it simply means that they should consider what the child prefers and why. This input may open parents' eyes to what their children are experiencing, and that information may be useful in guiding the parents to an appropriate timesharing schedule.

✷

We hope the above discussion of these ten major factors makes it clear why we cannot offer a single plan that would fit every family. Most families begin the divorce process with the premise that both parents should be actively involved in the lives of the children. Some parents, however, start the process believing that the children should be with one parent the vast majority of time. If the parents agree that both should be highly involved, we believe the parents should try to arrange for at least one third of the overnights to be spent with each parent. For many families, a 50:50 arrangement might function well, but it is not a magical formula. Sometimes a parent will become overly focused on what seems fair and strongly push for a 50:50 allocation of parenting time even when there are sound reasons why this might not be best for the children. We strongly advise parents to keep their focus on the children. Doing so may help resolve an impasse on this timesharing issue.

If the parents strongly disagree about the allocation of parenting time, they should seek assistance to work through their differences. A parenting consultant, a family therapist, or a mediator can guide the parents to a solution, and we encourage parents to engage these supportive resources to avoid the need to have a court decide the issue for them. These disagreements are more likely to happen in cases where one parent believes he or she should be with the children the vast majority of the time, but they can also happen when parents agree that each parent should be highly involved, but do not agree on the degree of that involvement.

Unfortunately, it is not always possible for parents to reach an agreement about the allocation of parenting time without the court's involvement. In such cases, the judge makes the final determinations about the allocation of parenting time. If it appears that the decision will be made by the court, the family may choose to have an evaluation done. This type of evaluation has been traditionally referred to as a *custody evaluation*, though the definition of custody can be ambiguous. Other terms for this type of evaluation are *timesharing evaluation* or *parenting plan evaluation*. These evaluations can be quite intensive and expensive and should not be undertaken unless there is a definite need. However, if it appears very likely that a case will go to court, an evaluation may be an effective way to provide the court with a large amount of objectively gathered, relevant data.

Determining the Timesharing Schedule

The allocation of parenting time is only one aspect of timesharing. Families also need to design a specific schedule for when the children will be under the care of each parent. No one schedule works for all, so parents must determine which schedule they believe is best for their family.

We like to use two-week blocks of time to explain timesharing schedules because they encompass alternating weekends, which is a nearly universal element of such schedules. To illustrate this point, consider a family that has chosen to use an *equal timesharing* allocation (i.e., 50:50 parenting time). This schedule, which has become more common in the United States over the past few decades, provides for each parent to have the children for a total of seven nights in a typical two-week period (see Tables 1 – 4). There are many ways that these seven nights might be distributed throughout the two-week period, and how they are distributed helps to define the schedule. We will start our exploration of timesharing schedules by looking at four equal timesharing schedules.

2/2/3 Schedule

We begin with what is referred to as a *2/2/3 schedule*. During the first week, the children are with Parent A for two nights, then with Parent B for two nights, and then with Parent A for three nights. The schedule alternates so that during the second week Parent B has the first two nights, Parent A the second two nights, and Parent B the final three-night period of the two-week sequence. Both three-night blocks include weekends that extend from Friday to Monday, allowing the parent who has responsibility for the children for that period to pick the children up after school on Friday and return them to school on Monday morning. This schedule prevents the children from being away from either parent for more than three consecutive overnights and provides a neutral location—the school or day care facility—for the transition from one household to another (during the school year). One downside of this schedule is that it does not provide consistent weeknights for the parents and children to be together (i.e., the children are with one parent on Monday and Tuesday one week and with that same parent on Wednesday and Thursday the next week), but that is not a major obstacle for most families. Another downside is that it requires six transitions (i.e., going from one parent to the other) every two weeks. Using the school as the point of exchange, however, lessens concerns about possibly awkward, tense, or hostile interactions between the parents.

Table 1. Example of a 50:50 Parenting Time Allocation with a 2/2/3 Schedule

	Mon	Tue	Wed	Thu	Fri	Sat	Sun
Week 1	A	A	B	B	A	A	A
Week 2	B	B	A	A	B	B	B

2/2/5/5 Schedule

The second schedule is referred to as a *2/2/5/5 schedule*. In this arrangement, the children are with one parent Monday and Tuesday nights, with the other parent Wednesday and Thursday nights, and with each parent on alternate weekends (see Table 2 below). One advantage of this schedule is that it is simple and offers consistency of weekdays for both children and parents. Another benefit is that it requires only four transitions every two weeks. The biggest downside of this schedule is that it results in a five-day block every week during which the children are away from one parent or the other. This extended period away from a parent may not be overly problematic for older children, but it tends to make the 2/2/5/5 schedule less ideal for young children. Some families mitigate the effects of the prolonged separation by including one or more formally scheduled daytime or dinnertime contacts in the middle of the five-day stretch.

Table 2. Example of a 50:50 Parenting Time Allocation with a 2/2/5/5 Schedule

	Mon	Tue	Wed	Thu	Fri	Sat	Sun
Week 1	A	A	B	B	A	A	A
Week 2	A	A	B	B	B	B	B

7/7 Schedule

The third schedule is a *weekly rotation*, i.e., alternating weeks (see Table 3). One good thing about this schedule is that it greatly reduces transitions, as there is only one transition per week. It is for this reason that, among 50:50 schedules, a 7/7 schedule is a useful option for older children, especially when parents are using an encapsulated co-parenting approach. By eliminating frequent exchanges, the potential for conflictual interaction drops significantly. This schedule is also more commonly used in families in which the parents live a greater distance from each other and exchanges involve a large amount of travel time for the children and the parents. Unfortunately, there is a downside to the 7/7 schedule; it means not seeing each parent for a week at a time, which poses difficulties for many children and is unacceptable for almost all young children.[6] Parents using a weekly rotation should consider including some midweek contacts between the children and the parent with whom they are not spending that week. These extra contacts are designed to help mitigate any negative effects from a parent's extended absence.

Table 3. Example of a 50:50 Parenting Time Allocation with a 7/7 Schedule

	Mon	Tue	Wed	Thur	Fri	Sat	Sun
Week 1	A	A	A	A	A	A	A
Week 2	B	B	B	B	B	B	B

---

6 As children's language and cognitive abilities, conceptual and emotional memories, and awareness of time develop and mature, they can better tolerate longer absences from a parent.

4/3/3/4 Schedule

A less common solution for equal timesharing that works for certain families is a schedule that has the children with one parent during most school nights and with the other parent during most non-school nights (see Table 4). We mentioned above that alternating weekends is an almost universal component of timesharing schedules, but for some families, alternating weekends is not feasible. A *4/3/3/4 schedule* might be well suited to a family's needs when one parent works every weekend and the other does not.

Table 4. Example of a 50:50 Parenting Time Allocation with a 4/3/3/4 Schedule

	Mon	Tue	Wed	Thu	Fri	Sat	Sun
Week 1	A	A	A	A	B	B	B
Week 2	A	A	A	B	B	B	B

Other Schedules

The following section applies to families in which there has been a decision for the children to spend more overnights with one parent than with the other. What we show in the heading of each table below is the number of overnights the child spends with each parent during a two-week period, so an 8:6 schedule has the children with one parent for eight nights in a two-week period and with the other parent for six nights in that same period. It is important to remember that these are just a handful of examples, and the range of possible schedules is extensive. As you look through these possible schedules, keep in mind this guiding principle: No one schedule works for all, so parents must design whatever schedule they believe is right for their family.

Table 5. One Example of an 8:6 Timesharing Schedule

	Mon	Tue	Wed	Thu	Fri	Sat	Sun
Week 1	A	A	B	B	A	A	A
Week 2	B	A	A	A	B	B	B

Table 6. A Second Example of an 8:6 Timesharing Schedule

	Mon	Tue	Wed	Thu	Fri	Sat	Sun
Week 1	A	A	B	B	A	A	A
Week 2	A	A	A	B	B	B	B

Table 7. One Example of a 9:5 Timesharing Schedule

	Mon	Tue	Wed	Thu	Fri	Sat	Sun
Week 1	A	A	A	B	A	A	A
Week 2	B	A	A	A	B	B	B

Table 8. A Second Example of a 9:5 Timesharing Schedule

	Mon	Tue	Wed	Thu	Fri	Sat	Sun
Week 1	A	A	A	B	A	A	A
Week 2	A	A	A	B	B	B	B

Table 9. One Example of a 10:4 Timesharing Schedule

	Mon	Tue	Wed	Thu	Fri	Sat	Sun
Week 1	A	A	B	A	A	A	A
Week 2	B	A	A	A	B	B	A

Table 10. A Second Example of a 10:4 Timesharing Schedule

	Mon	Tue	Wed	Thu	Fri	Sat	Sun
Week 1	A	A	A	B	A	A	A
Week 2	A	A	A	A	B	B	B

Once parents establish a regular schedule to address the days when children are in school, the next step is to begin to plan for sharing time during school breaks, holidays, and special days, as well as for accommodating family vacations. We will review these topics one at a time, starting with school breaks, which include the largest total numbers of days outside of the regular timesharing schedule.

Designating School Breaks, Holidays, and Vacations

School Breaks

School breaks are defined by the school calendar. In most places in the United States, school breaks occur in the spring, summer, and winter, with the latter occurring at the end of the calendar year. We will focus on these common breaks. Some families use the regular timesharing schedule throughout the year and do not apply a different schedule during any of the school breaks. The advantage of this approach is that the schedule remains consistent, but the disadvantage is that it may hinder either parent's freedom to travel with the children beyond the amount of time dictated by the established timesharing schedule. As a result, many families use different scheduling procedures for such times.

Parents sometimes alternate *spring break*, which is typically one week long. One way to do this is to allow each parent their usual weekend, but to alternate on a year-to-year basis the five weekdays that the children are out of school. Other families divide the break in half, with each parent having the children for four to five days straight. Some families choose for the children to be with one parent or the other for the entire spring break, including the weekends at both ends, which allows more time for travel. If the Easter holiday is important to parents, they will need to consider ways of dividing spring break that accommodates this holiday, as Easter Day falls during this break in many parts of the country.

Winter break, on the other hand, is usually two weeks long, and most families split that period in half so that each parent has a full week that could accommodate travel. Winter break includes Christmas, however, which means that dividing the break in half can create a challenge for parents who want to share that day with their children. Some families decide to alternate the Christmas holiday by year while others divide up the number of days in question and find annual work-arounds to carve out travel or other time that suits either or both parents. If a family celebrates Hanukkah, which often falls outside of the winter break, the family may be similarly creative and find ways to either divide or rotate the holiday. This same principal applies to all holidays that occur around the time of winter break.

Summer break is much longer, extending from the end of the school year in May or June until the start of the next school year in August or September, and it typically lasts about ten weeks.[7] Depending on a family's needs and the parents' preferences, summer breaks can be handled

---

7 Some areas in the United States now have year-round schools. These school systems do not have extensive summer breaks, but instead have more evenly divided breaks distributed throughout the year. The basic principles we discuss about school breaks still apply.

in numerous ways. Some parents simply continue with their typical timesharing schedule. Others maintain the same ratio of time, but they simplify the schedule and reduce the number of transitions over the summer. For example, a family with a 50:50 timesharing plan might shift from a 2/2/3 schedule (Table 1) to a 7/7 schedule (Table 3). This might better accommodate for spending time with out-of-town guests (e.g., grandparents or other extended family) or may simplify how the parents go about arranging summer enrichment programs for the children.

For other families, summer break days may be used to compensate for parenting time that one parent has sacrificed to accommodate the school year schedule. For example, a timesharing schedule with an uneven allocation of time may be used when one parent, Parent B perhaps, lives too far from the children's school to have numerous overnights during the school year, or is otherwise unable to accommodate frequent overnights on school nights. Over the children's summer break, the children could spend extra time with Parent B to balance out the amount of parenting time.

The schedule chosen for the summer break should accommodate each parent's desire for vacation travel with the children, and we will address the scheduling of vacations in more detail later in this chapter. We want to note here, however, that some families choose to divide the whole summer break in a manner that allows extended travel for one or both parents. If a family engages in prolonged periods of summertime away from home (such as spending a month at the grandparents' vacation home in the mountains or spending a similar amount of time traveling to visit family in India), parents might choose to divide the summer into two large blocks of time, during each of which the children will be with one parent. Such long periods away from parents during the summer would not be prescribed for most families, and especially not for younger children, as this arrangement leads children to be away from one parent or the other for a very long stretch of time. However, each family establishes its own culture, and parents need to develop a plan that is right for their children.

Holidays and Other Special Days

Families generally develop a schedule for where the children will spend certain holidays and other special days. Some days are too important to have the children's time be structured according to the regular timesharing schedule. For example, if the father regularly has a big family cookout on Memorial Day, and the mother throws an annual Halloween party for the neighborhood, these parents might specify that the children will be with the father on Memorial Day and with the mother on Halloween every year. Or, if both parents highly value watching the fireworks on the Fourth of July, the children might alternate this holiday between the parents. Family traditions are important for children.

The way a family handles holidays or special days is strongly influenced by their culture, faith, and traditions. While many of these days have deep significance in family life, we encourage parents to keep holiday scheduling as simple as possible. Shorter lists of holidays are better than longer lists. If a holiday or observance, religious or otherwise, is not truly important to the family, allow it to alternate naturally according to the standard timesharing schedule. However, if the event or occasion really matters to the family (taking into consideration that parents may have different backgrounds and family traditions), it should be specifically addressed. Some families might not include Presidents' Day, Fourth of July, and Halloween, for example, while other families might feel that one or more of these are essential. The choices for some special days may seem obvious, such as where the children should be on Mother's Day or Father's Day. Others may take some discussion, negotiation, and compromise in order to reach an agreement on whether and how they should be specified.

Once the family has specified the holidays and special days to be included, the next step is to decide whether to alternate, divide, or share them. The most straightforward way is to alternate each day that is important to the family, with one parent having the children in odd-numbered years for certain days and the other parent having them in even-numbered years for those same holidays or special days. Most parents set it up so that each parent will have the children for approximately half of the specified holidays in any given year. Alternatively, parents may choose to divide some days. i.e., the children will spend part of a day with one parents and the rest of the day with the other parent. For parents who use a cooperative approach, it may even be possible to share some days, i.e., the children participate in the main activity of the day with both parents. An example of this might be having the whole family meet for dinner at a restaurant on a child's birthday or participate together in Halloween trick-or-treating. As with all things in a parenting plan, the true goal is finding an arrangement that works for the children and is agreeable to both parents.

Many scheduled days off from school, such as federal holidays or teacher planning days, fall on Mondays or Fridays. One simple way to address these is to attach them to the adjoining weekend, which allows for a few three-day weekends for the children to be with each parent. But for some families, it is easier to just stay on the same schedule and not make a special arrangement for these days. When creating the plan, however, be mindful of how one decision might impact others. For example, if the typical two-week schedule has the children with the same parent each Monday, then that parent will periodically lose time if the children spend some Monday holidays with the other parent. This is only a few days each year, and it is certainly not enough to have an impact on a child's well-being. However, it can feel unfair to the parent who loses those days. An adjustment may be needed to account for this. The time to work this out is while developing the parenting plan, not after the fact when a parent later determines that this missed time is unacceptable. For days off from school that are not planned, such as snow days, we believe it is better for the children to follow the usual schedule unless the parents mutually agree otherwise.

An important special day to consider is a child's birthday. These are very special events, and most parents understandably want to enjoy some time with their child on the actual date. However, if the child has school that day, trying to divide the remainder of the day between parents while working around homework and bedtime may not be realistic or pleasant for the child. If the child has a summer birthday, dividing the day is easier, but if there are other children in the family with school-year birthdays, parents may want to consider whether handling those birthdays differently is a good idea. We recommend doing what most intact families do: Celebrate children's birthdays that fall on a school day by having a party the weekend before or the weekend after birthday. When the birthday falls on the weekend, celebrate it on the actual day. If parents get along well enough to attend a party together, they may choose to have a joint party. If the parents cannot be around one another without notable tension or arguments, however, they should alternate who will host the primary party, i.e., the party that includes the child's friends. The other parent may choose to host a smaller, family-focused party.[8]

Vacations

Vacation time is another item that the majority of parents choose to include in their plan, often designating that each of them may have at least one or two weeks of vacation time with the children. This period usually occurs during the summer, but parents may also choose to travel during their other school-break parenting times. In any case, we encourage parents with young children to limit the time the children are away from either parent to one week, whereas older children are able to tolerate longer blocks of time away from a parent. An uncomplicated way to schedule these vacations is to allow one parent to have first choice of his or her preferred vacation days in even-numbered years and the other parent to have first choice in odd-numbered years. The selecting parent, Parent A, for example, must notify Parent B of his or her preferred days by a specific date, and Parent B then has two weeks in which to select his or her vacation dates for that same year. The next year, Parent B would go first.

---

8 Having two separate birthday parties that include the child's friends can be awkward. If there are two distinct sets of friends, however, and each set is associated with a different parent, two primary parties might work.

There are times when the language used to describe vacation time has unintended consequences. For example, if parents alternate weeks, i.e., they have a 7/7 schedule, and they agree that during the summer each would take an additional week to create a fourteen-day period of uninterrupted vacation time with the children, they will find that they actually now have twenty-one-day periods with the children. The extra week they each take is sandwiched between weeks that the children already spend with that parent. Ideally, parents will be able to resolve problems like these when they arise, but it is best for them to proactively identify and address these issues when they are developing the parenting plan. In the above example, the plan might state that if one parent's vacation results in the children spending two weeks in a row with that parent, then the following week (i.e., the third week) will shift to the other parent, allowing each parent to have two consecutive weeks and avoiding long periods of time when the children are separated from the other parent.

It is also important for parents to clarify in their parenting plan how school breaks, holidays, and vacations will relate to one another, i.e., which ones have priority over others. If Parent A is scheduled to have the children over winter break and Parent B is scheduled to have the children for the first two days of Hanukkah, and the two coincide, which one prevails? If Parent B is scheduled to be with a child for the child's birthday, but the other parent's vacation week encompasses the birthday date, with which parent does the child spend his or her birthday that year? A simple statement written into the plan can define how they will resolve handling these days.

Exchanging the Children Back and Forth

Once it is decided how to devise a timesharing schedule that accommodates all of these considerations, there is one more group of issues to address: the when, where, who, and how of exchanging the children from one parent to the other.

The first issue is *when* the exchanges will take place. Parents must establish specific times that exchanges will occur for the typical, two-week schedule, as well as for all other exchanges—school break days, holidays, special days, vacations, and unplanned days off from school. Consistent times are easier for everyone to remember, so that is the approach that we recommend. Occasionally, however, circumstances will require unique arrangements or parents will have preferences that will guide the timing of exchanges in the parenting plan.

A second issue is *where* to make the exchanges. With younger children, if the parents get along reasonably well, the simplest and most natural place for an exchange is at the parents' homes. When children are in day care or school and the facility is in session, it is often best to have the exchanges take place at the start or the end of the school day so that one parent drops the children off and the other picks them up. Some families prefer to use a convenient, neutral location for exchanges when school is not in session, so a park or a local coffee shop is used as the place for exchanges.

In the arrangement outlined above, the parents must also make a third decision: *who* has responsibility for the children after Parent A has dropped them off at school and before Parent B has picked them up. For example, if the child gets sick and needs to go home, which parent is responsible for providing care? A viable approach would be the following: Arbitrarily designate either the drop-off or the pick-up time as the *official* exchange time so that it, in turn, can dictate which parent is responsible for the child. In other words, if the official exchange is designated to occur at the time of the drop off, then the parent who is scheduled to pick up the child is responsible for the child during the school day. If, on the other hand, the pick-up time is designated as the time of exchange, then the parent who dropped the child off in the morning continues to be responsible during the school day.

Another consideration regarding school-based exchanges, however, is that they do not easily accommodate the transfer of belongings. Parent A, for example, may have to either deliver the children's property separately to Parent B or allow Parent B to retrieve the needed property from Parent A's home. A helpful solution can be having two sets of essentials (pajamas, toothbrush, etc.) at each home. This does not eliminate the need for some transfer of belongings, but it limits it.

The fourth consideration is *how* the exchange will take place when there is a higher level of conflict between the parents. For families with higher levels of conflict, exchanges that cannot take place at school or day care need to occur at a public location that is sure to have other people present, such as a fast-food restaurant or a town library. If there is any concern about violence, the exchanges might have to take place at a police station or other law enforcement facility, or they might need to involve a neutral third person, such as a family member or friend on whom both parents agree. (These options apply primarily to families that require an encapsulated co-parenting approach.) As awkward as it may be to conduct exchanges at locations outside of the home or school, this may be necessary to protect the children from their parents' verbal or physical violence. These conditions are also sometimes needed to ensure that parents do not engage in hostile conversation at exchanges.

In this chapter and the previous one, we have reviewed two major components of a parenting plan: decision making and timesharing. There are, however, other elements of a parenting plan that need to be addressed as well. Those elements are discussed in the next chapter.

nine

The Parenting Plan: Everything Else

Beyond decision making and timesharing, there are other less weighty considerations that are also important to a parenting plan. Combined, these other elements constitute perhaps only a quarter of the whole plan, but they can be critical in helping parents manage their co-parenting relationship and prevent future disputes. The authors have each worked with families for whom major decision making and timesharing were easily established, only to find that one or more of these other elements were difficult to resolve. In most cases, however, once decision making and timesharing are settled, the remaining items are fairly easy to negotiate.

Information Sharing

One issue to consider is how parents will share information about the children. Even if one parent is the sole decision maker, both parents should have access to all information pertaining to the children in areas such as education and health care. Access to information should also mean allowing both parents to confer with anyone who is a service provider to the children, such as doctors, teachers, or coaches. Unless there is some major reason not to do so, parenting plans usually require that both parents be listed as emergency contacts for the children on any school, day care, summer camp, or provider records.

Beyond each parent having access to information, parents bear a responsibility to keep one another informed of key information regarding the children. Ideally, this can occur in an easy and frequent manner. However, in families where there is pronounced parental conflict, or if one parent tends to harass the other, the way they share this information may need to be limited and strictly defined, though it must still take place. (Email, which provides written documentation of the communication, is a tremendously useful option for these families.) In more contentious cases, it is best to prohibit phone communication, except in the case of a legitimate emergency.

Parent-to-Child Communication

The parenting plan must also address parent-to-child communications to specify how frequently and by what methods the children will contact a parent when the children are with the other parent. Some parents and professionals believe that it is important for children to speak with each of their parents every day. Others feel that contact between the children and the parent who is not providing care to them on a given day is unnecessary and may, in fact, be intrusive or disruptive to the other parent's time with the children. If daily calls can be made between the children and that parent without causing undue tension within either household, then we think it is a very positive and healthy routine to establish. In some families, however, phone calls may remind children of how much discord there is between their parents. If these calls lead to an escalation of conflict or hostility, or if they cause anxiety or stress for the children, then the parents should establish a less frequent pattern of communication. To find a reasonable balance between allowing daily contact with each parent and not allowing calls to be intrusive, parents may consider the following: On days when the children do not see one of the parents at all (i.e., days when there is no exchange), the parent caring for the children will make sure that a call is placed at the end of dinner or some other specified time. This approach ensures that the children have contact with each parent each day, but also reduces the overall number of phone calls.

Even when calls are made according to the schedule, parents sometimes perceive that the other parent is not trying hard enough to facilitate the calls or is actively interfering them. While this might be true in some cases, it should not be assumed that this is case just because the calls do not go well. There are times when children—as much as they may love a parent and enjoy being with him or her—find a phone conversation tedious, and they desperately try to avoid it. Younger children are generally not capable of sustaining lengthy phone calls, or even calls lasting more than a few minutes. We suggest that the expectation for the length of the calls be tied to the maturity of the children and the children's proven ability to sustain a call. There is no need for long calls with younger children. With younger children, the parent at home with them should be responsible for making the call and staying present until the call is completed. With older children, the parent who is caring for them should remind the children to place the call, and if necessary, personally observe that the call was initiated. The parent should then allow the child to speak with the other parent without monitoring the conversation itself. Another way of initiating calls with the children is to make an arrangement that the parent who is not with them will call at a specified time.

Child Care

Another common element spelled out in parenting plans is an agreement surrounding child-care providers such as nannies and babysitters. In some plans, parents are allowed to unilaterally select providers, while other plans require that parents mutually approve of all child-care providers. Parents sometimes agree to include in their parenting plan that either parent may select any babysitter *except* one or more specified people, such as a friend or relative who has been actively involved in the parental conflict. Some parents agree that neither parent will use a male babysitter with a daughter. All of these agreements must be included in the parenting plan in order for them to be formalized as rules that the parents must then follow.

Many parents include in their plan a clause that provides each parent with the option to accept or refuse the opportunity to care for the children before a child-care provider is engaged. This is known as the *right of first refusal*. For instance, if the father must be away from the children for a designated period (e.g., six hours or more) during his parenting time, then he is required to contact the mother and offer her the chance to supervise the children personally, rather than having the children in the care of a babysitter. The mother may agree to provide care for the children for those hours, or she may decline the right to do so, in which case the father is responsible for arranging for a babysitter.

A four-hour right of first refusal is not uncommon with small children, but that time frame usually becomes too short as children get older, so many parents prefer to use six, eight, or ten hours as the minimum amount of time before triggering the right of first refusal. A shorter time frame requires parents to interact more frequently, which can be disruptive to the children and dilute any benefits that might have been gained from extra parenting time with the other parent. Some families limit the right of first refusal to situations in which a parent will be away from the children overnight, and some families simply choose not to include a right of first refusal in their plan at all.

We would suggest that the higher the level of conflict between the parents, the higher the threshold should be before the right of first refusal is activated. In other words, with severe conflict, if a right of first refusal is to be specified at all, it should only be for overnight or all-day absences. In all parenting plans, the right of first refusal clause should have an exception to allow for children's planned social opportunities, such as spending an overnight with a friend, going on an overnight scouting trip, or having special time with grandparents.

Travel

Parenting plans should also include rules about traveling with the children. Parents may treat certain types of travel differently. The three types of travel to be considered are in-state, domestic (i.e., in the United

States as a whole), and foreign travel. The vast majority of families with which we have worked have allowed in-state travel without requiring specific permission, though parents are required to notify each other of such plans. For other domestic travel (i.e., out-of-state travel within the United States), the approach is more evenly mixed. Many families we have seen do not require explicit permission, but some do. Either way, the traveling parent must provide the other parent with advance notification of the dates of the trip and a reasonably detailed itinerary, including flight numbers and times, locations where the children will be during the trip, and a contact phone number. International travel may be more complicated for some families, especially if there is genuine concern about possible abductions (such as when one parent has extended family in another country and has expressed a wish to relocate to that country of origin) or when a parent has not had a good track record of ensuring regular communications during absences from the other parent.

School Selection

Another key element in parenting plans is deciding where the children will attend school. Unless the plan identifies a specific site, it is necessary to include a statement as to which parent's address will be used to determine the child's assigned school. In general, when the children spend the majority of school nights with one parent, it makes sense for the children to attend a school nearer that home. When parents have equal timesharing, the children may continue at the schools that they are currently attending, or the parents may include a provision in the plan that the children will attend the highest-rated school that is near one of the parent's homes. Since the locations of the parental homes may change over time, defining the process used to determine the schools is arguably more important than simply selecting a specific school. Many parents do both: They identify the specific schools the children will attend, but also specify how schools will be selected if circumstances change, such as if a parent moves out of the school catchment area.

Handling Disputes

One final but essential consideration to address in the parenting plan is how to proceed if there are disputes about the implementation of the parenting plan. If the parents have already selected a professional to help them work on co-parenting matters, then they may choose to commit themselves to asking that professional to help resolve any conflicts that arise in the plan's implementation. If the parents do not currently have a co-parenting professional, then they might simply state in the plan that they agree to use a yet-to-be-determined consultant should the need arise. Finally, some parents include a statement in their plan that says that before filing a court action, the parents will use a mediator, parenting coordinator, or other type of professional consultant to try to resolve the conflict.

❧ ❧

A question is often raised about how detailed a parenting plan should be. If parents get along well and both tend to be very reasonable with one another (i.e., if the level of conflict is low), a more basic plan may suffice. In higher-conflict families, we advocate for a very detailed plan. Details, if carefully considered and carefully worded, can save a great deal of time, money, and stress down the road. We think that the best approach for most families is to have a moderate amount of detail, somewhat more than might seem necessary and thus enough to provide guidance should unexpected disputes arise. We believe that a useful motto when designing parenting plans is, "Simplicity with clarity." For example, it is important to designate pick-up and drop-off times and a standard pick-up location to avoid any confusion about when and where exchanges will take place. Similarly, if you agree to a summer program for your child, you should specify who will pay for what, who will provide transportation on which days, who will provide which supplies, and how the schedule of the program might relate to the timesharing schedule. The point is that a good plan provides enough information to guide both parents without requiring ongoing negotiation.

Once all of the above sections of the parenting plan are decided upon, the next step is to draft it. A parenting plan must be drafted, at the latest, before the final judicial hearing because it will become part of the marital settlement agreement or final judgment of the court. Whenever possible, however, we recommend that parents draft a temporary parenting plan at the time they separate. If it is a trial separation, the plan does not need to elaborate. If the separation signifies the end of the marriage, however, the temporary parenting plan should be fairly detailed. When a temporary plan is in place, it helps to guide the parenting efforts of each parent during the stressful period before the marriage is dissolved, and it provides an opportunity to test the agreements in the plan before committing to them on a permanent basis.

The parenting plan may be written by any of the following:

- The parents
- The attorneys
- A mediator
- A parenting consultant
- The judge

If the parents have been able to work out the issues on their own, they may choose to write the parenting plan themselves. Usually, parents are able to access self-help forms that guide them by offering a series of options from which the parents may choose. Parents also benefit from reading handouts, webpages, and books about parenting plans (such as this very book).

Many times attorneys prepare parenting plans on behalf of their clients. Some attorneys are better informed than others about the crafting of child-centered parenting plans. We encourage parents to keep their attorneys aware of their desire to place the children's needs above other factors when drafting these plans. This also applies when a mediator is involved. If mediating, the specific wording of the parenting plan should be discussed during the mediation session. The degree to which the parenting plan is child-focused will depend on how clear the parents are about the elements they want to include in the plan and the particular wording that they choose.

Having a parenting consultant involved may be the best option to guarantee that the plan is child-centered. Parenting consultants are almost always mental health professionals who have extensive training and experience in child development, and who can thus help parents understand their children's developmental needs. The resulting document is more likely to reflect those needs and to fully prioritize the interests of the children.

Finally, when a judge writes a parenting plan, it may provide some customization to accommodate individual families, but will probably result in the least tailored parenting plan of all. One reason for this is that judges are responsible for overseeing all of the issues involved in the divorce, so they are rarely in a position to devote the hours needed to craft a unique and detailed plan for each family. In addition, judges generally have very limited interaction with the parents.

One approach that some families use to manage costs while also accessing guidance is for parents to draft the parenting plan as far as they are able after reviewing sample parenting plans and reading relevant materials. They then seek out a mediator or a parenting consultant to help them work through the remaining conflicts and develop a final draft. The parents can then have their attorneys—if they have retained attorneys—review the plan.

It is very important that parents recognize that developing a thoughtful, family-specific parenting plan takes time and effort. While parenting plans can be negotiated and prepared in one sitting, such as during a mediation session, we believe that creating the parenting plan should be a process rather than a one-time activity. Part of that process should involve the parents becoming educated about co-parenting issues and allowing enough time to carefully consider each of the many options from which they will have to choose. From our perspective, the decisions that are involved in the development of the parenting plan will almost certainly have an enormous effect on the quality of the children's and parents' lives for many years to come. Critical decisions deserve time and due diligence. We also believe that it is vitally important for parents to have substantial input into the writing of the plan, as that input gives the parents a sense of ownership over the final document. This, in turn, will make a tremendous difference over the course of time in the parents' investment in—and compliance with—the parenting plan.

ten

Keys to Mindful Co-parenting

In this chapter we want to have a very direct conversation with you. This is the same frank and pointed conversation that we have with parents in our offices when they ask us how they might best assure their children's emotional well-being through the course of a divorce. Much of this has been touched on in previous chapters, but now we will discuss what we believe are the key factors that represent the heart of mindful co-parenting.

Each of these factors relies on your intention to live mindfully. By tuning into your deepest values and staying aware of your experience in the present moment, you make it possible to accomplish each of these co-parenting tasks. As an example, you are much more likely to be able to communicate effectively or manage your emotions if you are paying attention to what is happening within you at that very moment. These six factors are interrelated, as each one helps you to achieve the others. Those who maintain boundaries, for example, find it easier to follow agreements and to focus forward. While some of these objectives might require great effort, we encourage you to pursue them all to the best of your ability. You will find that success in one leads you to succeed with others. Each of them plays a critical role in helping you create an emotionally healthy environment for your children even in the midst of your divorce.

Keys to Mindful Co-parenting

1. Putting the children first

2. Focusing forward

3. Communicating effectively

4. Honoring agreements

5. Maintaining boundaries

6. Managing your emotions

Putting the Children First

Putting the children first means making a conscious and committed effort to always prioritize your children's needs. We are not suggesting that children should get everything they want, but rather that their needs be carefully contemplated in each and every situation. For example, if you know that your co-parent is planning to drive straight from your house to take your son to a friend's birthday party at 1:30 p.m., it seems evident that it is in your son's best interest to make sure he has his lunch _before_ 1:30 p.m. Doing so not only addresses your son's immediate need of having lunch, but it also prevents conflict with your co-parent who might otherwise be frustrated by having to stop to get lunch on the way to the party. Similarly, if your co-parent is twenty minutes late for a planned pick-up time, it is clearly better for your daughter if you wait until later to address the matter with that parent, rather than starting an argument in front of your daughter.

There are several reasons why parents lose sight of this objective and make choices that are not in their child's best interests. When parents are very angry with each other, that anger may cloud their judgment and lead them to act out against one another despite the collateral damage the children might suffer. Sometimes parents also lose sight of their children's best interests simply because they themselves are overwhelmed, confused, exhausted, depressed, or otherwise worn down. In such cases, parents may have trouble thinking through the impact of their actions on their children. We encourage you to try seeing each situation through your children's eyes, paying attention to their feelings and preferences even when they interfere with your own. When the balance has to tilt in one direction or the other—toward what is best for your children or toward what might be best for you as a parent—we strongly recommend that you tilt it toward your children. Putting your children's needs first is a central tenet of mindful co-parenting.

Part of prioritizing your children's needs means concentrating on those goals that you and your co-parent have in common. We presume that you both love your children and are committed to their well-being. We also presume that you can agree on certain goals regarding their upbringing, such as having your children achieve academic success or ensuring that they receive particular religious training. If you both foster those goals, then you are working on a shared agenda that will advance your children's interests. Simply by working together and guiding the children in the same direction, you are giving your children one of the gifts of effective co-parenting.

Another aspect of putting your children's needs first is to do everything possible to insulate your children from your co-parenting conflict. It is not realistic to think that all parents will resolve the negative feelings they hold toward each other, but children should not be exposed to ongoing disputes between parents. Children can understand and accept that their parents do not agree about some issues and that their parents are trying to work those out, but parents should not share the details of their legal battles with their children, nor should one parent make allegations against the other in front of the children. And, without a doubt, children should never have to witness verbal or physical confrontations between Mom and Dad. Children have a big enough job just learning how to live in the world; they should not have to deal with their parents' battles with each other. In families of divorce, children face plenty of challenges associated with living in two homes and having two parents who may not like or respect each other. It only makes things worse if you let your conflict spill over onto them. Arguments between Dad and Mom concerning divorce issues are not something to which the children should be subjected, and keeping them free from the conflict is one very powerful way that you can put your children first.

Focusing Forward

Drivers who focus their attention on what is behind them are more likely to collide with objects in front of them. A similar phenomenon happens far too often with parents in a divorce. By focusing on the conflicts and emotional injuries of their broken marriage, parents are distracted from the important tasks involved in caring for their children. They carry the past into the present, and this results in very negative consequences for themselves and their children. By holding on to grievances from your marriage, you may seriously hinder your co-parenting relationship.

Focusing forward is essential because the quality of your co-parenting *today* relies on it. Unless you focus forward, you will derail your interactions with your co-parent by dwelling on what happened—or what you *believe* happened—in the past. You will have a hard time making agreements that pave a new path for you and for your children, and you will continue to be enmeshed in disputes that are based on lingering hurt, anger, and resentment.

We recommend that you focus on a best-possible future, not on winning battles that originated in the past. You cannot change what already happened. If you have old issues that need to be resolved, try working through them by having a calm but honest discussion with your co-parent, either independently or with the involvement of a divorce therapist or similar counselor. If your co-parent is not willing to address those issues in a productive way, however, then the only option is to let go and let the past be the past. That may not seem fair, as you may believe that doing so lets your co-parent off the hook for previous misbehavior, but it is important for you and your children that you move on. You may feel an urge to vent your frustration, but venting is not as helpful as you may wish to think it is. Venting to your co-parent may be cathartic, but it will not change the other parent and it will not change the past. In many cases, in fact, it just exacerbates the conflict and makes things worse. If you must vent, do it with a friend, a therapist, or just about anyone else other than your co-parent.

In addition to letting the past go, it is helpful to learn to let go of minor issues arising in the present. For example, suppose that you want your children to eat a healthy dinner every day, but your co-parent takes them out for fast food at least twice a week. You wish you could convince your co-parent to do otherwise, but this may be something that you simply cannot change. If the co-parenting relationship can handle it, and if you have reason to believe that your co-parent might consider your wishes, go ahead and present your case. Explain your concern — then let it go! You may not want your children to have so much fast food, but that burger and fries will not be as damaging to them as increased parental conflict will be. Focus on the big issues, especially those you have reason to believe you can and should affect, and let the smaller ones slide. It is not worth a lot of time or energy to wrestle over whether your co-parent returns the children's extra underwear that you bought, or whether your co-parent signed a permission slip for a field trip without asking you. If you want to address the issue, ask your co-parent, in a neutral tone and with reasonable expectations, to handle the situation in a different way going forward. Whatever the outcome, let it go and move on. If there is an ongoing pattern of these types of behaviors by your co-parent, then obviously there is a larger issue that needs attention. But occasional missteps on the part of your co-parent do not have to be addressed. Pick your battles.

You have a choice: You can stay in a constant struggle or you can accept your co-parent's shortcomings and make it work as well as it can. This requires you to accept that your children's lives will not always be as easy or smooth as you would like for them to be. It may be helpful to remember that even if you and the children's other parent were still married and living together, life would not be perfect for you or for your children. Now that you are apart, there is more need for compromise and acceptance, and that requires that you abandon some of your expectations. If you feel that you always take the high road and your co-parent never does, we assure you that you are not the first to experience this. You may compromise far more often than your co-parent does, and you may, in fact, accommodate many special requests only to have your one request refused for no good reason. But before you start drawing lines in the sand and engaging in escalating conflict, ask yourself this question: *Which choices will serve my children?*

We acknowledge that asking you to let go of frustrations of the past and present may seem unfair, and we understand that there may be moments when you will wish you could punish your co-parent. However, we suspect that if you are being mindful—in this case, if you are paying attention to what you truly value—you are willing to shoulder more than your fair share to protect your children. Regardless of what happened in the past, even in the very recent past, you have the freedom to focus forward and to approach each decision with an awareness of what your children need today.

Communicating Effectively

Even under ideal conditions, effective communication is not easy. If you add in strong emotions, harsh negative biases, and a difficult relationship history, it is much harder. The ability to communicate effectively with your co-parent, however, is essential. This is true whether you like each other or not and whether you plan to interact frequently or infrequently. Communication is necessary because co-parents must share information about the children, and in most families, must make certain decisions together. You simply cannot complete these tasks if you are unable or unwilling to communicate with one another.

Co-parents can communicate in a variety of ways. Some parents are able to talk effectively in person, while others prefer to speak by phone. Moderate-conflict families may limit their primary communications to email and texts, with occasional face-to-face or phone contact as needed. Higher-conflict co-parents often rely exclusively on email, which provides digital documentation of the communication and helps to prevent an escalation of conflict. The box below contains guidelines that we recommend for all parents whenever they use email as a method of communication.

Email Guidelines

◊ Keep all emails brief and to the point.

◊ Be respectful and polite.

◊ Leave out personal opinions, criticisms, demands, threats, or sarcasm.

◊ Offer solutions that your co-parent might find agreeable.

◊ Read and edit the message carefully before you send it.

◊ Reply within a pre-agreed time frame (a 24-hour reply time is common).

◊ Ask yourself, "Will sending this email make my children's lives better?"

There are some co-parents whose level of conflict is so high that they are not even able to manage direct email communication. These parents may use a communication website through which their messages to one another are monitored by a parenting coordinator or other court-affiliated professional. There are a number of websites that offer a range of services for nominal fees. Many include a shared calendar, systems for exchanging the children's school or medical records, and message programs that maintain a reviewable history of the communications between the parents. If necessary, printed documentation of these communications can be provided to a designated professional or the judge overseeing the case.

Regardless of whether communications between co-parents are spoken or written, they should always be respectful. There is no place for hostile, attacking, threatening, coercive, abusive, badgering, harsh, or accusatory statements, and we strongly advise parents to make an absolute commitment to never resort to using these types of comments with one another. Communication should also be as pleasant as reasonably possible. We picture a continuum of acceptable tones of communication that extend from cooler to warmer, as seen here:

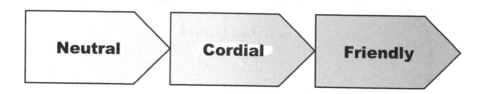

There is no warmth in a *neutral* tone, but neither is there any negativity or hostility. While we consider a neutral tone to be adequate, it is not the ideal tone for co-parents, so we encourage them to try for something beyond this level. A *cordial* tone is a step above neutrality, as it adds a layer of courtesy, such as greeting the other parent at an exchange of the children, addressing the other parent by name, and using the words "please" and "thank you" as appropriate. A good example of a cordial tone is an email that you might send to a customer service representative when you are asking for assistance in resolving a problem. You address the person politely, you state your requests in a straightforward manner, and you conclude with an appreciative comment. Most parents can achieve a cordial tone, even if it requires some effort. We recommend that parents do everything in their power to maintain at least a cordial tone.

The warmest tone in this continuum is a *friendly* tone, and this is one that many divorced parents cannot sustain. For those who can adopt this option, however, friendliness takes the level of warmth a step beyond cordiality. When you are using a friendly tone, whether you genuinely like one another or not, a person overhearing you would assume that you are friends. They would perceive at least some warmth and caring about one another, and they would hear some casual, spontaneous comments. While children do not need their parents to be friendly, it does benefit the children by creating a more relaxed and mutually supportive environment. Think about it from your child's perspective: How might you feel if you saw your parents communicating without any warmth (neutral tone), with politeness but limited warmth (cordial tone), or with ease, openness, and warmth (friendly tone)?

Beyond the factors above, there are other ways to make your communication more effective. We encourage parents to always follow the three Cs:

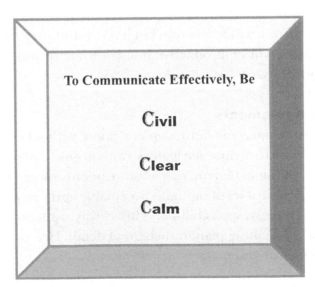

To Communicate Effectively, Be

Civil

Clear

Calm

The first of the three C's is being *civil*. Civility is expressed in tone, so this first item follows from our discussion above, and even a neutral tone qualifies as being civil. The second of the three C's is being *clear*. For example, if you were communicating with a business associate, you would be brief, but descriptive, to help him or her understand your perspective, and you would stay focused on the message to avoid unnecessary commentary. In turn, you would listen patiently to the reply and consider it thoughtfully before responding. We recommend that you apply this same clarity with your co-parent. The third C is being *calm*. No matter how a business associate spoke or acted, you would strive to remain relaxed, reasonable, and rational. You would manage your emotions and you would manage your outward demeanor even if that person said something that upset you or that you believed to be untrue or unkind. You would be the one responsible to keep yourself in check regardless of how he or she behaved. Maintaining calmness around your co-parent can go a long way toward preventing conflicts and containing them when they occur.

These various communication guidelines may not always be easy to follow, but even when they are not easy, you can follow them. Optimizing your communication is important, so we urge you to manage the content and the tone of your communication, and to follow the three Cs in all of your dealings with your co-parent. Doing so may not guarantee that your co-parent will follow suit, but it is certainly more likely that the communication will be productive if at least one of you sticks to these recommendations.

Honoring Agreements

A building contractor cannot erect a house without clear blueprints from an architect. Airline navigators cannot guide pilots without detailed maps. In the same vein, co-parents can only succeed at co-parenting when they have a set of mutually acceptable agreements that outline their co-parenting responsibilities. This is why we have discussed the structure of a parenting plan in such great detail. Here we will focus on the importance of *honoring your agreements*.

Extending the above metaphors, if a contractor ignores blueprints or a navigator does not consult maps, problems will ensue. Once a well-designed plan is in place, it is essential that each co-parent stick to every agreement. The only exceptions are when both parents agree to an alternative plan regarding some particular matter. You cannot control the other parent, as we discuss later in this section, but you can make sure that *you* honor all agreements. For example, if you have a parenting plan that requires you to bring the children back at 5:00 p.m., then bring them back at 5:00 p.m.—not at 5:10 p.m. If the agreement states that you will notify your co-parent at least three days before traveling, notify your co-parent as soon as possible, but no less than three days ahead.

Honoring agreements means not only adhering to the letter of the agreement but also doing your best to honor the intent. A carefully written parenting plan will cover all of the main issues that are likely to arise in the course of co-parenting, but no one can anticipate every possible circumstance. A parent who searches for loopholes in the parenting plan and exploits those loopholes may be adhering to the strict instructions, but he or she is not truly honoring the agreement. Co-parenting has a higher purpose than just following rules. While a court may insist that you abide by the written word of the parenting contract, we hope that you will be mindful that your goal is to work with your co-parent in raising your children. Abide by the rules, but also be respectful of the overall intent of the agreements.

There are several different reasons why a parent may not comply with an agreement. A parent may refuse to comply because he or she does not fully understand the agreement, or because he or she interprets it differently from the other parent. Politely explaining your understanding of the agreement is a good first step, and that may be enough to solve the problem. If it does not, a co-parenting professional may be helpful in getting both parents to better understand and accept the agreement as written. If the problem is that the parenting plan is inadequately detailed, the professional might also help by assisting the parents in adding sufficient detail or clarity to the plan.

Sometimes parents refuse to comply because they are in a power struggle. There are also parents who try to manipulate the agreement in their favor. (This includes the parents we referred to above who seek to exploit loopholes in the written agreement.) A failure to abide by an agreement can also result from a parent facing an obstacle that he or she has not yet resolved. For example, if your co-parent is always fifteen minutes late for exchanges, and it turns out that being late is because his or her new boss will not allow any employee to leave work early, you could remove the obstacle by simply adjusting the exchange time or moving the location to one that is more accessible to that parent's workplace. In some situations, the only way to achieve compliance is by thinking outside the box and finding a creative way to get around the obstacle:

> *Jennie regularly picked up her son, Jimmy, at 5:30 p.m. for two hours of parenting time on Tuesday and Thursday evenings, but she never seemed to be able to bring him back to Ed's house until close to 8:00 p.m. By the time she would take Jimmy to her house and feed him his dinner and work with him on his homework, they would have to get back in the car to go to Ed's. Ed suggested that Jennie take Jimmy to a restaurant and do his homework there, but Jennie told him that she can't afford to eat dinner out twice a week.*
>
> *Jennie came up with the idea of bringing a picnic dinner that Jimmy can eat at a recreation center near Ed's house where she and Jimmy can also work on his homework. But she then realized that this wouldn't be feasible because she picks up Jimmy at Ed's house on her way home from work, so she would not be able to prepare an appropriate meal. Ed, however, loves to cook, and he offered to have a well-prepared picnic meal ready for Jennie and Jimmy to take with them at the exchange. Jennie agreed to try it and it worked out well.*
>
> *By considering this creative and cooperative solution, Jennie and Ed removed the obstacle that caused Jennie to bring Jimmy home to Ed's house late, and from that point on she was very*

punctual in regard to the 7:30 p.m. drop-off time. Ed went out of his way to help her and she is likely to remember this, which may lead her to be helpful to Ed in other co-parenting situations in the future. Most importantly, Jimmy witnessed this cooperative spirit and now feels better about how Mom and Dad get along.

As this example illustrates, you may be able to gain your co-parent's compliance by asking *in a non-accusatory way* what it is that makes it hard to comply and then working together on a solution. If you can identify the obstacle, you might be able to find an easy fix. Another approach to gaining compliance is to enlist the help of people whom your co-parent knows and trusts. Mutual friends, a well-respected neighbor, a clergy member, or family members with whom you both still have a good relationship—any of these might be good candidates to help encourage your co-parent to do the right thing by honoring agreements. We have even seen cases in which a co-parent's dating partner or new spouse was enlisted to help, although this obviously requires that you have an amicable and trusting relationship with him or her.

A variety of professionals may play a role in helping to facilitate compliance. If your child sees a therapist, that therapist might be more persuasive than you in convincing your co-parent to comply with the parenting plan for the sake of your child. If a *guardian ad litem* (a court appointed child advocate) has been appointed, he or she might be able to do the same, as might your attorney by communicating with your co-parent's attorney. Finally, parenting coordinators are excellent resources in this regard, as their role is specifically geared toward gaining and monitoring such compliance.[9]

---

9 For example, a parenting coordinator might remind a parent that the parenting plan is a legal document that serves as their guide for what must happen. The only exception to adhering to the terms of the plan is when the parents mutually agree to some alternative arrangement. If a parent continues not to comply, the parenting coordinator may need to report this to the court. At best, this can take a lot of time and involve otherwise unnecessary expense. Further, judges typically are not happy that a parent has refused to follow a clearly stated court order and sometimes respond to this rather harshly.

If all else fails, you may decide to take your co-parent to court. We do not propose this lightly. In our opinion, going to court should always be a last resort, the thing that you do when you have tried every better way to resolve a problem and the problem still needs fixing. The one argument in favor of going to court is that if nothing else works, it may solve the dilemma—but there are significant downsides. First, any time you file a motion against your co-parent, you are likely to get pushback and hostility. Second, going to court is costly, and if you use an attorney to represent you, it can quickly become very expensive. Third, going to court is stressful, and it will consume a great deal of time and energy on your part. Fourth, courts are often overbooked, so you need to anticipate a potentially long delay in getting to a resolution. Fifth, you may invest all the time and money required and still not have things change. Last, resolving an issue via the court may open a proverbial can of worms, as other unresolved issues may now become points of contention and litigation. All of this is *not* to say that you should never go to court to enforce an agreement. Rather, we are suggesting that you should try other approaches first and then consider if the likely benefits of going to court outweigh the likely costs. If so, then it may be the step that you need to take. Most judges are pleased to know that you have already attempted other methods to resolve your disputes, so trying other things first is a good idea, even if you are confident that you will ultimately need to bring the matter before the court.

There is one final alternative for when your co-parent is not complying with your agreement: Do nothing. If his or her resistance affects an important aspect of the parenting plan, such as refusing to honor the timesharing agreement, making major decisions on his or her own, or violating the parenting plan in a way that endangers the children, then doing nothing is not an option. If the area of noncompliance is minor, however, you may decide that it is better to let it go. Keep in mind that doing nothing means tolerating the violation, not resolving it. If that will work for your children, then it may be something to consider. These are decisions that you will want to discuss with your attorney and with any other parenting professional with whom you are working. You do not want to inadvertently establish a precedent of not expecting or requiring compliance, but you must balance those concerns against choosing your battles wisely. As we have pointed out time and again, making wise, mindful decisions is critical.

Maintaining Boundaries

One of the key tasks of co-parenting is establishing and maintaining clear boundaries—i.e., respecting one another's space, time, new relationships, privacy, career, financial situation, and so on—is essential. Boundaries protect both parents by allowing each of you to function in your own lives without the other's presence in non-child-related parts of your lives. Maintaining boundaries also protects your children from the tension and conflict between parents that might result if you were to intrude into each other's lives. You share your children, but the other areas of your lives should not be encumbered by your past or present connection to your ex-spouse.

As we discussed above, one of the most important ways to safeguard boundaries so that they are not violated is by adhering to agreements, including the parenting plan. The parenting plan, as well as any written agreements that are developed after that plan is signed, create boundaries in the co-parenting relationship. By honoring your agreements, you are honoring the boundaries in your co-parenting relationship.

You can also observe boundaries by stepping back from any efforts to control your ex-spouse's parenting choices. Thoughtful, respectfully conveyed feedback to your co-parent may be well intended, but you need to be careful not to cross the line. It is one thing to offer constructive feedback to your co-parent, and it is another thing to point out that he's a lousy father who is immature or she's a terrible mother who is selfish. We understand that you may not fully trust your co-parent's judgment, such as when she lets your eight-year-old stay up until midnight on weekends, or when he plays violent video games with your ten-year-old. It would certainly be appropriate to discuss your concerns about these matters, but how you go about that can make all the difference in regard to whether it will increase or decrease the level of conflict. If you demand change with guns ablaze, you will get more resistance than if you have a calm and polite conversation about the advantages of consistent bedtimes and limits on the amount of violence to which your child should be exposed.

You need to make choices about how much influence you will attempt to have over your co-parent's parenting style. If you attempt to micromanage your co-parent, you are bound to get resistance. Instead, we encourage you to allow some latitude and save your constructive comments for those issues that are high priorities. For example, looking again at the bedtime scenario, if your child functions reasonably well even with a later bedtime on non-school nights, then this might not be a problem. On the other hand, if your child always returns from your co-parent's home tired and unable to function the next day, or unable to fall asleep the next school night, then this might warrant discussion. The overriding goal is to be mindful of whether your input is necessary and appropriate. Too much input, or poorly offered input, is likely to disrupt the reasonable boundaries that exist between you as co-parents and thereby increase the level of conflict. A measured amount of input, offered in a respectful, collaborative manner, will offer a better chance at resolving your concerns while reducing the likelihood of conflict.

Boundaries are not static and they may change over time. At certain points in your co-parenting relationship, it may be necessary to have more rigid boundaries so that one or both parents can adjust to a co-parenting relationship that is fundamentally different from the relationship that existed during the marriage. Early in a divorce, when parents are learning how to relate to one another as co-parents rather than as spouses, it is often necessary to adhere to stricter, clearer boundaries. As time passes and co-parents adjust, they often find they can soften their boundaries because there is less risk of igniting the types of conflicts that were present during the marriage and the divorce process. In other cases, however, boundaries need to remain firm on a long-term basis. When there has been a history of abusive behavior or domestic violence, for example, it is essential that the boundaries stay solidly in place for many years and in extreme cases, perhaps forever.

Managing Your Emotions

One of your greatest responsibilities in co-parenting is figuring out how to manage your own emotions through the twists and turns of divorce. This is not an easy task for most people. Divorce draws out a wide range of emotions, and co-parenting disputes can fuel this process for years beyond the final court hearing. Nevertheless, learning how to manage your emotions is critical to succeeding in co-parenting. Fortunately, there are several ways to develop these skills.

How you think about your relationship with your co-parent can actually play a very big role in helping you manage your emotions. If you can stay mindful of the fact that you are no longer emotionally connected to each other, but instead are functioning as a team working on a very important joint project, you will be much less likely to slip into conflict. It is completely understandable that strong negative emotions exist during and after a divorce, especially when the divorce was triggered by hurtful, selfish, or destructive behavior on the part of at least one of the parents. However, you are not required to like each other, or even respect each other, in order to behave responsibly and cooperatively (although it does make it much easier if you do like or respect each other). Regardless of the feelings you have about one another, you are forever connected by being the primary parents of your children and by being the two people in the world who most love these children and want the best for them.

There are other ways in which you are connected by your children as well, such as through family, friends, and all of the support people in your children's lives, including pediatricians, clergy members, teachers and school personnel, as well as your children's friends and their parents. Recognizing all of these types of connections may help you to avoid viewing your co-parent as an enemy, and instead allow you to see your co-parent as a difficult-to-deal-with but important person. This shift in perspective may, in turn, help you to manage your emotions when interacting with your co-parent.

We understand that no matter how hard you try, there will be times when you will find yourself in a dispute with your co-parent. At those times, we urge you to do everything in your power to resolve your differences without escalating the dispute to a higher level. Find a way to stay calm so that you can handle the matter maturely and responsibly, no matter how angry you might feel. Do not yell, do not threaten, and do not violate any agreements just because you are angry. Avoid filing motions in court or having your attorney send nasty letters just because you are frustrated. Try your best to work it through by communicating with your co-parent calmly, and if need be, meet with a neutral professional, such as a parenting coordinator or a mediator, to resolve the issue. If even that does not solve the problem, you may need to involve your attorney, but make sure your attorney understands that you want to resolve the issue, not start a war. Look at all options for collaboration and cooperation. If the issue needs to go to a judge, so be it, but always look for ways to resolve the conflict rather than to escalate it.

Admittedly, it can be difficult for any of us to handle our emotions when a dispute gets intense. That is especially true when dealing with an ex-spouse, or a soon-to-be ex-spouse, who may have done many hurtful and selfish things. It is even more difficult if that ex-spouse is still making your life miserable today. As hard as it may be, one of your tasks as a divorced parent is to figure out how *not* to act out on your emotions within your co-parenting relationship. It is essential that you manage your emotions and your actions, and part of this is learning not to take the bait when your co-parent tries to engage you in conflict. Your co-parent knows how to push your buttons and is not afraid to do so—and may, in fact, be very motivated to do so. Your co-parent may provoke you for a variety of reasons:

- For revenge
- To escape from a losing argument
- To protect his or her image by making you look like the angry, irrational one
- For his or her own entertainment
- To feed a desire for control
- Out of habit, as old habits die hard

Whether your co-parent intentionally or unintentionally antagonizes you, your job is to find the "off switch" for that button. Your objective is to find a way to keep from reacting reflexively. Your co-parent may want to set you off, but you do not need to indulge that desire.

Another way to reduce conflict is to treat your co-parent with good faith, decency, and politeness. You help no one, including your child, if you behave with animosity or aggression. There is never a good reason to be cold, rude, sarcastic, harsh, demeaning, provocative, or dismissive. It serves no worthwhile purpose to stonewall, attack, or in any other way make life difficult for your children's other parent or stepparent. Every unhelpful action you take can have a harmful effect on your children, whether or not they directly observe it. Our advice is to stay on the right side of all of this; that is, behave in a way that you can be proud of and that protects your children's interests. The right side refers to being decent and respectful, trying to work with your co-parent, and showing a willingness to cooperate to resolve problems rather than just create problems. The courtesy and cooperation that you demonstrate will hopefully result in more courtesy and cooperation in return, at least over time. Remember, even if your co-parent does not display the same goodwill toward you, your commitment to walk the line and behave honorably will serve your children's interests while you maintain your integrity.

≫∽≪

This chapter has addressed the factors that we believe are the keys to mindful co-parenting. We hope that you will see them as straightforward, even if they are not always easy to apply. We cannot overemphasize the importance of making these a part of your daily life as a divorcing or divorced parent. Even under the very best of circumstances, co-parenting can be a tough job. When you add in higher levels of conflict and intense emotions, especially when you are involved in litigation, the challenge can seem monumental. The good news is that when you are willing to do so, you and your co-parent *can* learn how to work as a team for the sake of your children. This is true even when you are unable to get along well with one another and even when you have deep animosity toward each other. By using mindfulness as a foundation, and attending to the above factors as guides, you and your co-parent can lead your children on a gentler path through divorce and beyond.

eleven

New Romantic Partners and Blended Families

Sooner or later, one or both parents will probably start dating. Moreover, statistics on second and third marriages clearly indicate that one or both parents will remarry or will at least live with a new "significant other." The entry of new adults into your life and into your children's lives is something that the vast majority of families should expect. It can bring both challenges and joys. Our focus here, as it has been throughout the book, is to help you use a mindful approach to minimize the difficulties and maximize the rewards.

We will begin with romantic partners. We expect that most parents will have an interest in dating at some point in the future. At the right time, this can be a very healthy thing, but when one parent is ready sooner than the other, the less-ready parent may feel hurt, angry, and resentful. You may be that not-so-ready parent, and we understand your struggle. At the same time, you cannot expect your co-parent not to date just to spare your feelings. Likewise, you should not deny yourself the opportunity to date in order to keep your ex-spouse happy or unperturbed. Dating is likely to happen, and it is best to acknowledge it and to deal directly with whatever feelings you may encounter. By facing the reality and acknowledging your feelings, you free yourself up to focus on how these changes will affect your children.

Introducing the person you are dating into your children's lives should be done gradually and with very careful consideration of your children's needs. The common advice, which we endorse, is to wait a reasonable period of time until a dating relationship becomes more serious before introducing your dating partner to the children. No matter how wonderful this new romantic partner may seem, and no matter how sure you are that this is "the one", you need to give the relationship time. You cannot be sure how things will work out. Many relationships that seem perfect at the start turn out to be disappointments or mistakes just a few weeks or months into them. For this reason, we recommend that parents not introduce new romantic partners to their children until they have dated the person for at least four to six months. We also recommend that parents allow their children at least four to six months to adjust to the idea of their parents' divorce prior to meeting new romantic interests. Thus, if you began dating someone before your children knew about the divorce, we would use the latter date (i.e., the date they found out about the divorce) as the starting point for counting the four to six months. We acknowledge that there is no exact science to these time frames. Each family is unique. But we believe these are reasonable and practical amounts of time, as they allow parents to be mindful of their children's needs while also accommodating their own needs as unmarried adults.

Another major issue to consider is whether romantic partners will stay overnight in the home while the children are there. For some parents this is absolutely unthinkable; for others, it may seem self-evident that this will occur. This decision has to do with personal values and your expected time frame for remarriage. If the parents disagree about this, it is important they try to find mutually acceptable solutions and boundaries. If the parents are going to have overnights with romantic partners while the children are in the home, we strongly recommend that this not occur until at least a year of dating has elapsed *and* until the children have known this dating partner for at least several months *and* until the children appear to be comfortable with that person's role in their lives.

These guidelines may seem restrictive to a newly single person, but the goal is to protect children from being exposed to a series of different romantic partners and having to adapt to adults who enter and then disappear from their lives. Additionally, these losses may come relatively soon after your children have already worked to make sense of other significant losses: of their intact family, of consistent time with each parent, and possibly of their familiar home or neighborhood. You cannot protect your children from all of these losses, but you can avoid exposing them to some additional ones, and your good decisions about not involving a romantic partner prematurely can spare them from unnecessary distress. Be patient so that you do not compromise what is best for your children as you meet your own needs.

A particularly important issue to consider is what role your romantic partner will have in regard to your children's daily lives. As with all things, this will depend on the particular circumstances within your family, but there are a few rules of thumb. First, during the early interactions between your romantic partner and your children, the partner should not be a disciplinarian but should instead simply be present as a caring adult. When the romantic relationship becomes more committed, the interactions between the children and your partner will need to evolve. The parent and his or her new partner should discuss their expectations with one another about how much the new partner will be involved in parenting tasks. If the romantic relationship goes from dating to living together to marriage, there will be adjustments at each of these stages.

When you have found the right person, and you have given the relationship enough time to become a committed one, you may decide to live with that person even though you are not married. You and your new partner need to carefully consider how you plan to handle your partner's entry into the home. It is your home, but it is also your children's home. Having a live-in partner is further complicated, of course, if your new partner also has children who will be blending into the home and into the family. (We will touch on this issue further when we address stepsiblings.)

Once your new partner becomes more involved in your life and your children's lives, you will need to consider how to create the most helpful (or the least harmful) relationship between your ex-spouse and your new partner, bearing in mind that both are key players in your children's lives. We have met families in which ex-spouses and new partners develop friendly, supportive relationships, which is a wonderful and welcome outcome for everyone. Sadly, however, we have also seen families in which they degenerate into bitter enemies who use the children as pawns in a battle for control.

If you are not the one with the new relationship, but your ex-spouse is, how might you react? Would you feel jealous, threatened, or resentful about having a new adult in the lives of your children, or would you experience a sense of relief that your ex-spouse has moved on? These are useful questions to ask yourself before you find yourself in a situation that might raise these feelings. Exploring them in advance might also sensitize you to how your co-parent might feel if and when you are the one to begin a new relationship.

In time, you or your co-parent will likely make a decision to become engaged to a new partner. Of course, deciding to remarry is not only about you. Having a stepparent inserted into their home and lives can be very difficult for some children. If that stepparent has children who also reside in the home full time or part time, the situation becomes even more complex. While blended families have become commonplace in our society, they are by no means simple, and we encourage parents to approach the joining of families with the same mindful approach we have advocated throughout this book.

Being an effective stepparent is not an easy task. Many people find that it goes more smoothly with younger children and older adolescents than with the in-between age groups. Younger children tend to be more accepting of new adults in their lives, especially if the adults are encouraging, warm, and fun. Older adolescents tend to develop a different quality of relationship with their stepparents. These teens are likely to have started to form their own identities and may be less invested in integrating into the stepfamily. Nonetheless, stepparents can play a meaningful role for these adolescents as supportive adults who may be freer than the primary parents to fill a non-confrontational mentoring role.

In many families, preteens have the most difficulty integrating with a stepparent and stepsiblings. These younger adolescents are just learning who they are and how they fit in to other groups including the family. A new authority figure in their lives, one about whom they may be ambivalent, can be very confusing and threatening. A stepparent should be aware of this dynamic and take steps to fulfill his or her role in a way that minimizes a young teen's sense of being unreasonably monitored or controlled by yet another adult.

Stepparents should be cautious about trying to establish themselves as new parents to the children. We encourage them to move slowly and to let each child's needs and responses determine the pace. Be available, be kind, and be patient. Even under the best of circumstances, newly formed stepfamilies may require several years to work through the adjustments of living together and defining their new roles and relationships. Over time, as the children adjust to the new family structure, the stepparent can start to take on more of the parental tasks.

In some blended families, after the family has integrated, a stepparent may be as involved, or even more involved, in daily parenting tasks than the primary parent in the home. This is because, in many respects, they are serving as a surrogate for the primary parent in the home and may spend more time with the children than the primary parent does. In these cases, there may be disputes regarding the extent of the stepparent's role, especially concerning his or her child-related supervising, disciplining, transporting, or day-to-day decision making. The other primary parent may also have concerns that the stepparent is supplanting him or her. And there may be truth to this in some families; when a stepparent is heavily involved, the role of the same-gendered primary parent can weaken, especially if the relationship between a child and that primary parent is already compromised.

Another common issue that arises in regard to stepparents is how the stepchildren address them. Some stepparents like to be called Mom/Mommy or Dad/Daddy, but most families choose to reserve these titles for the primary parents. It can be helpful to find meaningful yet different titles for stepparents. Some families opt for adding a first name, such as Mommy Susan or Daddy Mike. If everyone finds that acceptable, then there is no problem, but many families find such a nickname is still too close to Mommy or Daddy to feel comfortable. Many families use only first names for the stepparents, especially when the family is blending at a time when the children are older. None of these options are inherently right or wrong, but it is important that both primary parents are comfortable with the titles that are used.

Blended families may include both stepsiblings and half siblings. Much as stepparents may play valuable roles in children's lives, stepbrothers and stepsisters, as well as half brothers and half sisters, can add a whole new layer of richness to children's lives. Along with these benefits, however, come challenges. Almost by definition, when a family blends, the parents in that family are committing to sharing their time and resources with all of the children in the household. That can cause tensions when children have to share their own parent with their new stepsiblings. This same issue can occur when a new baby is born into the family and that child becomes the center of attention. Children may also struggle with their new family life when they do not get along very well with their stepsiblings. The good news, however, is that most children ultimately establish a positive relationship with their stepsiblings and can become as close as biological siblings who have grown up together.

One further challenge regarding blended families is the sense of split loyalty the children may experience. They may reject the stepparent out of a sense of allegiance to their primary parent of the same gender. On the other hand, children often come to love their stepfamily to such an extent that they feel guilty about having these feelings, or they are in-secure about expressing them. This is especially true when there is con-flict between the primary parents, or when the children perceive one of their primary parents to be unhappy, hurt, or angry. Most children work through these feelings, but they need support and assistance in doing so. We encourage parents not to hesitate to give children the chance to speak with a counselor to help address these feelings after a divorce.

twelve

A Few Final Thoughts

We are hopeful that this book has resonated with you. If so, we are confident that you are committed to finding a child-friendly path through the process of divorce and beyond, and that bodes well for your children. Before wrapping up this book, though, we want to briefly address two more matters that we believe deserve attention. First, we want to identify several special circumstances for which additional help will be needed. Second, we want to highlight the importance of parents finding the support that they might need to most smoothly navigate the challenges of divorce for themselves and their children.

Special Circumstances

While the vast majority of families facing divorce can resolve their own issues, there are some circumstances that pose unusual challenges. Among these are severe parental conflict, allegations of child abuse, extreme rejection of a parent by a child, and doubts of one parent regarding the ability of the other parent to adequately meet the needs of the children. When a family faces one or more of these issues during or after a divorce, they are very likely to need additional help in the development and implementation of their parenting plan. They will also almost assuredly need added resources to help with the co-parenting relationship.

Severe parental conflict most often occurs when one or both of the parents have a personality disorder that leads to volatile, manipulative, selfish, inflexible, or otherwise unreasonable behavior on a regular basis.[10] Severe parental conflict is distinguished from high conflict by the depth and breadth of the problems that it causes. While high conflict can sometimes be managed by the parents themselves (though often these parents choose to obtain additional help), severe conflict is extremely difficult to contain and almost always requires professional involvement. In Chapter 6 we discussed the benefits of applying an encapsulated co-parenting approach with these families. If you believe that your co-parenting relationship falls within this difficult area, we encourage you to review that material and seek appropriate assistance. Severe conflict is damaging to everyone in the family.

Allegations of physical, sexual, or emotional abuse of a child create another circumstance that compromises the ability of parents to work together. This is true whether the allegations of abuse are based in fact, are the result of a misperception, or are a manipulation and untrue. When any suspicion or allegation of abuse arises, it is essential that the child be properly evaluated without delay. Any required reporting to the appropriate agencies should occur immediately, and then an evaluation by a licensed provider who specializes in these types of evaluations should be conducted. When inadequately trained or inexperienced professionals are engaged to do these assessments, errors may occur that lead to a failure to identify real abuse or a failure to expose false allegations. Delays may compromise the reliability of information, especially information obtained directly from a child. A delay may also leave a child in an abusive environment, which is the greatest concern of all. The possibility of abuse demands careful, vigilant, and prompt attention.

---

10 A personality disorder is an enduring psychiatric condition that can usually be traced back to a person's adolescence or early adulthood. There are different types of personality disorders, but the most common ones cause problems both for the individual and for others. People with personality disorders persistently engage in maladaptive behaviors that occur in a wide array of personal and social settings.

A third circumstance that raises complex issues is when a child rejects spending time with one parent or begins to view that parent in a highly negative light. In the more severe cases this is referred to as *estrangement* or *alienation*. If the rejection is based on real-world factors, such as that parent acting in an unloving or uncaring manner or being unavailable to the child, then the solution would center on that parent's acceptance of the source of the problem and his or her motivation to change. In some cases, however, the rejected parent experiences more rejection or hostility from the child than would be explained by that parent's behavior. In these cases, the actions of the other parent or of other people in the child's life may play a role in negatively influencing the child. Cases in which the child refuses to see one parent and expresses great hostility toward that parent tend to be very difficult to resolve, even with professional intervention. A key to success is the ability of both parents to understand the dynamics that are causing the problem and the importance of resolving them. This is a complex undertaking that requires professionals with special training and experience.

A final special circumstance is when one parent deeply doubts the ability of the other parent to adequately meet the needs of the children. Despite their love for their children, some parents are simply ill-prepared for providing competent parenting. In some of these cases, the parent has not been highly involved in the children's care and may simply require time and experience to develop the necessary skills. In other cases, however, it may be a lack of effort or commitment rather than a lack of parenting ability. Some parents can be quite competent for hours at a time but lack the motivation or willingness to invest the time and energy that sustained good parenting demands. There are also parents who are unable to ensure the children's well-being as a result of those parents' serious mental health problems, such as major depression, bipolar disorder, severe anxiety, post-traumatic stress, or other psychiatric conditions. A parent who struggles with substance abuse or other addictions, has severe anger or impulse control problems, or a personality disorder may have a hard time consistently prioritizing the needs of the children over his or her own needs or desires. Any of the above conditions can interfere with a parent's decision making and judgment regarding the children. The more severely impaired a parent is, the more likely that the family will need professional assistance and the more likely that the court system will need to make certain decisions for the parents in order to protect the children.

Sometimes one parent distrusts the ability of the other parent to meet the needs of the children even though both parents are actually functioning reasonably well. These concerns may result from the first parent's misperceptions about the second parent, or they may stem from the first parent's anxiety in general about the children's safety or daily care. The circumstance that we see most often is one in which both parents offer adequate, but not equivalent, care for the children. One parent may be very alert and attentive to the children's needs, while the other parent is only moderately so. In these cases, the issue is really about the *relative* parenting performance of the two parents, and the problem to solve is not a *parenting* problem, but rather a *co-parenting* problem.

A common pattern that occurs is when a less attentive parent suggests that the other parent is spoiling the children and making them dependent or lazy, while a more attentive parent suggests that the other parent is reckless and neglectful. If one or both parents feel strongly that the other parent is being harmful to the children, then the matter must be addressed. It may be difficult to determine where the truth lies without a thorough assessment by a parenting professional. There are two likely outcomes for these types of assessments. If the concerns about inadequate parenting are reasonable and based on a true failing by a parent, then intervention should center on improving the skills of the parent in need. If the concerns about parenting are not reasonable, then the resolution should focus on helping the concerned parent begin to view his or her co-parent more realistically. The best course of action might also include having both parents agree to follow certain guidelines to protect the children from potential risks. Even if the risks are small, there is no harm in finding non-invasive ways of reassuring an overly worried parent as long as both parents find this tolerable.

While we hope that this book will be helpful to the majority of readers, we acknowledge that families that face the types of extreme challenges discussed in this section will require resources that go far beyond what this book can offer. To those families, we strongly recommend the involvement of professionals who specialize in the appropriate areas of evaluation and treatment. While these circumstances are difficult to address, the ultimate outcome for the children can be favorable when at least one parent takes the steps needed to get the children and the family the intervention that they deserve.

Finding Support

It helps to have help. No one is an island; most of us do better when we seek out guidance and support. In fact, social support has been shown to enhance our ability to cope with a vast array of psychosocial problems. There are no prizes for doing it all on your own, especially when there are so many potential sources of support available, each of which offers unique benefits. Most people going through a divorce do not need a team of professionals to be involved in their lives. They just need to be mindful about their decisions and their behavior and to reach out to their already existing social network.

Your natural support network may include members of your family, your friends, and possibly some of your coworkers, neighbors, and members of your place of worship. Telling your network about your divorce while it is happening is a good way to open the door to support. You do not need to wear your heart on your sleeve, but it is useful to cue people in to what you are going through. From there, you will find that a great deal of genuine caring will flow. Not everyone in your life will react in helpful ways, but those people who are your true support group will lean forward and lend a hand or offer a helpful word. When you need something beyond what they are offering, ask for it. Many people will spontaneously know what to say or do, but others who truly care may need a little prompting. Not everyone in your informal network will serve the same role or fit into your inner circle. You will find, however, that it is exceptionally helpful to have a few people with whom you can share everything that you are going through. These few, special people are your confidants. They comfort you when you are distressed, offer advice when you are uncertain, and support you in the choices that you make. Select them carefully—and then use them generously when you need them.

Another source of support can be found in organized peer groups for divorced parents. These groups may have a therapeutic focus or they may be more socially oriented, but they offer a concentrated form of interpersonal support that is often exceptionally helpful, especially early in the divorce process. Support groups generally meet on a regular basis, perhaps weekly or monthly, and they are usually offered at minimal or no cost. One limitation of divorce support groups is that they are not always readily available. They may be hard to find in some cities and may not be available at all in some rural areas. One alternative that has become widespread is online support groups. While these have the advantage of accessibility, they sacrifice the face-to-face experience that a local group offers. Still, organized peer-support groups for divorced parents are a valuable resource for many people.

We urge you to consider professional support when it is needed. Divorce is not an easy journey, especially when children are involved. Difficult journeys demand skillful guides. An attorney can be invaluable resource as you move forward. Other professional help is available from psychotherapists, child psychologists, parenting coordinators, and clergy and pastoral counselors, among others. A little bit of professional counsel can save a great number of missteps and much unnecessary suffering. Our advice is to seek an appropriate consultation when challenges are outside your range of experience or expertise. Even a brief session can provide useful information. From there you can consider whether it will make sense to engage that person to serve a greater role in helping you or your children.

There are two types of professionals who may be especially helpful in guiding you to become a mindful co-parent: divorce counselors and parenting coordinators. Divorce counselors are psychologists, social workers, marriage and family therapists, or other mental health professionals who specialize in providing counseling and therapy for children, adults, and families going through a divorce. They focus on helping you work through your feelings of anger, hurt, fear, and guilt so that you are able to function better on your own and relate with your ex-spouse in a healthier way. When working with children, divorce counselors help children identify and express their feelings, and they may help children and parents communicate more fully and more productively with each other. These counselors tend to work with families with low-to-moderate levels of conflict. Parents immersed in a high-conflict divorce process tend not to be interested in changing their feelings toward their ex-spouses and therefore are generally less willing to participate in any form of therapy.

It is these antagonistic divorces that bring parenting coordinators into play. Parenting coordination is a service that has grown rapidly in recent years and has now become the go-to approach for very high-conflict families in which there are minor children. The court appoints the parenting coordinator, often at the request of one or both of the parents, but sometimes at the sole discretion of the judge. The coordinator is typically a licensed mental health professional who has received training in mediation and conflict management. The court appoints the professional to help parents learn how to work better as a parenting team, and he or she may employ a wide range of techniques to achieve this goal. They include education, mediation skills, coaching, and persuasion, as well as the leverage that comes with being empowered, through a court order, to communicate to the court regarding the parents' participation. Parenting coordination cases can be very challenging, as they involve, by design, high-conflict couples. Even so, we have seen parents make remarkable changes in the quality of their co-parenting relationship. Parenting coordinators can also serve an important role by monitoring the parents, holding them accountable for their behaviors, and keeping both parents on track.

ᷖᴥᴖ

At some point in the process of your divorce, you begin to establish a new normal. The transition is over. Despite the challenges, most families find that they can succeed quite well over time. We have seen many, many parents rise up to meet these challenges and create a truly child-friendly family even in the midst of divorce.

Engaging in mindful co-parenting is a big part of realizing this goal. It does not happen on its own; instead, it takes time and effort to bring your co-parenting relationship to the best place it can be. We fervently believe that if you stay in touch with what really matters and are attuned to your children's needs, the path becomes clear. By devoting yourself to a mindful co-parenting approach, you give your children their best chance to grow up to be happy, healthy, and productive adults.

About the Authors

Jeremy S. Gaies, Psy.D., is a clinical psychologist and family mediator who works in private practice in Tampa, Florida. He earned his undergraduate degree from Brown University and his graduate degree from Rutgers University. Dr. Gaies specializes in helping parents navigate a peaceful path through and beyond divorce. His primary areas of practice are parenting coordination and collaborative divorce.

James B. Morris, Jr., Ph.D., is a clinical and forensic psychologist who works in private practice. He has offices in both Clearwater and Tampa, Florida. He earned his undergraduate degree from Florida State University, his graduate degree from the University of South Florida, and completed his residency and a postdoctoral fellowship at the University of Virginia. Dr. Morris specializes in helping divorcing and divorced parents effectively co-parent and in conducting parenting plan evaluations.

Made in the USA
Middletown, DE
02 September 2020